PREFACE

This study is based on open source research into the scope of organized crime and terrorist activity in the Republic of Mexico during the period 1999 to 2002, and the extent of cooperation and possible overlap between criminal and terrorist activity in that country. The analyst examined those organized crime syndicates that direct their criminal activities at the United States, namely Mexican narcotics trafficking and human smuggling networks, as well as a range of smaller organizations that specialize in trans-border crime. The presence in Mexico of transnational criminal organizations, such as Russian and Asian organized crime, was also examined. In order to assess the extent of terrorist activity in Mexico, several of the country's domestic guerrilla groups, as well as foreign terrorist organizations believed to have a presence in Mexico, are described. The report extensively cites from Spanish-language print media sources that contain coverage of criminal and terrorist organizations and their activities in Mexico.

TABLE OF CONTENTS

KEY FINDINGS

❖ Mexico's drug trafficking and alien smuggling networks have expanded their criminal activities aimed at the United States by capitalizing on the explosive growth of trans-border commerce under NAFTA and the attendant growth in human and merchandise traffic between Mexico and the United States. The growth in trans-border commerce, as manifested in soaring levels of overland passenger and commercial vehicle traffic, has provided an ever-expanding "haystack" in which the "needles" of illicit narcotics and illegal aliens can be more easily concealed.

❖ In the wake of the September 11, 2001 terrorist attacks on the United States, increased border security measures temporarily heightened the risks of interdiction for Mexican drug traffickers and alien smugglers. This heightened level of risk forced smugglers to increase their reliance on sophisticated counter-detection measures, such as border tunnels, multiple repackaging of drug shipments, containerization, and rail transport.

❖ Mexico's three major drug cartels are being superseded by a half-dozen smaller, corporate style, trafficking networks. In a process that mirrors the post-cartel reconstitution of drug trafficking networks in Colombia, this "new generation" of Mexican drug traffickers is less prone to violence and more likely to employ sophisticated technologies and cooperative strategies. The processes that are driving Mexican drug trafficking organizations toward establishing cooperative networks of increasing sophistication and decreasing visibility are likely to intensify in the post-September 11 environment. As a result, Mexican drug trafficking networks are likely to emulate their Colombian counterparts by investing heavily in counterintelligence, expanding and diversifying their legitimate enterprises, and concealing transnational partnerships that could attract undue attention from U.S. intelligence and law enforcement agencies.

❖ Alien smuggling from Mexico to the United States is a US$300 million-a-year business, second only to Mexico's illicit drug trade in terms of revenues from criminal activities. Between 100 and 300 human smuggling rings operate in Mexico, many of which are loosely coupled with one or more of a half-dozen core human smuggling networks that have extensive transnational contacts.

❖ A variety of Russian criminal organizations, operating through dozens of small cells, are engaged in a wide range of illegal activities in Mexico. Some Russian criminal organizations based in southern California have entered into drug trafficking partnerships with Mexican drug cartels.

❖ Asian criminal organizations are active in Mexico as partners with domestic alien smuggling and human trafficking rings, as suppliers of primary materials for narcotics to Mexican drug traffickers, and as wholesalers and retailers of counterfeit merchandise and pirated intellectual property.

❖ Between 16 and 25 domestic insurgent groups operate in Mexico. Except for the Zapatista National Liberation Army, none of the groups numbers more than a few dozen guerrillas. Their influence is largely confined to the southern states of Guerrero, Oaxaca and Chiapas, although some groups have perpetrated small-scale terrorist attacks in Mexico City and other urban areas.

❖ During the late 1990s, the Revolutionary Armed Forces of Colombia (FARC) established a clandestine arms smuggling and drug trafficking partnership with the Tijuana-based Arellano Felix Organization (AFO).

❖ Since the mid-1990s, Mexico, at the request of the Spanish government, has deported scores of terrorists belonging to the Basque separatist group, Fatherland and Liberty (ETA).

❖ Statements by high-ranking Mexican officials prior to and following the September 11, 2001 terrorist attacks indicate that one or more Islamic extremist organizations has sought to establish a presence in Mexico.

INTRODUCTION

Since 1999, trans-border criminal organizations based in Mexico have adapted to meet a variety of opportunities and challenges. Mexico's drug trafficking networks, in particular, consolidated their position as the primary suppliers of Colombian cocaine and other illegal narcotics to the western and midwestern United States. They were aided in this endeavor by the explosive growth of transborder commercial activity under the North American Free Trade Agreement (NAFTA) and the attendant growth in human and merchandise traffic between Mexico and the United States.

For Mexico's drug and alien smuggling networks, the growth in trans-border commerce, as manifested in soaring levels of overland passenger and commercial vehicle traffic, has provided an ever-expanding "haystack" in which the "needles" of illicit narcotics and illegal aliens can be more easily concealed. According to U.S. Department of Transportation statistics, the annual number of truck crossings from Mexico into the United States grew from 2.8 million in 1994 to 4.3 million in 2001.[1] Along the Texas border, the number of trucks entering from Mexico doubled in the span of a year, from about 1 million in 1997 to more than 2 million in 1998.[2] At the same time, the spread of the Internet, the proliferation of sophisticated encryption technologies, and the expansion of legal money flows between the United States and Mexico provided ample opportunities for the repatriation and laundering of drug profits earned in the United States. These trends made Mexico an increasingly attractive base not only for its domestic criminal groups, but also for a growing array of transnational criminal enterprises looking to expand their operations in the Western Hemisphere.

From the perspective of Mexico's trans-border criminal networks, favorable trends in the expansion of commerce were counterbalanced by an increasingly hostile political climate. In December 2000, Mexico's political system was transformed by the election of President Vicente Fox Quesada. Fox, the first opposition leader elected president since the Mexican Revolution of 1917, had run on a platform that included "war without mercy" on organized crime. Over the course of the next two years, the Fox administration's anti-crime program would result in the death or capture of dozens of high-ranking kingpins from all Mexico's major drug trafficking

---

[1] U.S. Department of Transportation, Bureau of Transportation Statistics. <http://www.transtats.bts.gov>
[2] Texas Center for Border Economic Enterprise Development, "1990-2001 Truck Crossings into Texas from Mexico." <http://www.texascenter.tamiu.edu>

organizations, as well as the disruption of dozens of criminal networks entrenched within every level of government, the military and law enforcement agencies.

During 2001 the Fox administration launched an unprecedented offensive against Mexico's drug trafficking networks. The Arellano Felix Organization (AFO), the largest and most sophisticated of the Mexican cartels, received the brunt of the blows. Taking advantage of the pressure being placed on the AFO, rival drug bosses, most notably Ismael "El Mayo" Zambada García, began to encroach on traditional AFO strongholds in northwestern Mexico. By the spring of 2001, Zambada was embroiled in a full-scale gang war with the Arellano Felixes.

The United States' response to the September 11, 2001 terrorist attacks was a temporary setback for trans-border Mexican criminal networks. The complete shutdown of U.S. southwest border stations for several days, followed by the imposition of more stringent border controls and a general decline in trans-border vehicular traffic, posed new challenges to Mexico's drug and alien smuggling organizations. As the risks of detection grew, Mexican drug traffickers and alien smugglers resorted to more sophisticated concealment methods, such as narco-tunnels, containerization, multiple repackaging and re-routing of drug shipments, and rail transport. Faced with a surplus of un-exported cocaine and marijuana, Mexico's drug barons sold more of their inventory to local distributors catering to a growing domestic market. As a result, local drug retailing organizations, such as the "Neza cartel," grew considerably in 2002. Finally, increased border security may have spurred an already existing movement into highly profitable and more easily concealable synthetic drugs, such as methamphetamine and MDMA (ecstasy), both of which are also popular in Mexico's resort areas.

During the spring of 2002, the Arellano Felix Organization (AFO) appeared to be in retreat, stung by the loss of kingpins Benjamin and Ramón Arellano Felix, the arrest of nearly 2,000 operatives on both sides of the U.S. border, and opportunistic attacks by rival drug lords. A U.S. law enforcement official compared the troubled AFO to the bankrupt energy firm Enron, saying: "Investors don't want to put money into a company if they don't think they'll get their money back. All of a sudden, AFO looks like a pretty bad investment, just like Enron."[3] Other major drug networks, such as the Juárez-based Carillo Fuentes Organization (CFO) and the

---

[3] Gretchen Peters, "US, Mexico Finally Drug-War Allies: President Vicente Fox's Unprecedented Cooperation with the US Yields Big Blows to Latin Narcotraffickers," *Christian Science Monitor,* 9 July 2002, 1.

Matamoros-based Cárdenas Guillén Organization (CGO), were also disrupted by law enforcement efforts.

The power vacuum left by the decline of the AFO is being filled by smaller Mexican drug trafficking organizations operating under what appear to be a new set of Fox-era and "post 9-11" ground rules. These organizations are less prone to violence and more likely to employ sophisticated technologies, such as advanced encryption and financial management software, secure Internet communications, chemical engineering skills, and advanced botanical know-how.[4] The processes that are driving Mexican drug trafficking organizations toward establishing cooperative networks of increasing sophistication and decreasing visibility are likely to intensify in the post-September 11 environment. As a result, Mexican drug trafficking networks are likely to emulate their Colombian counterparts by investing heavily in counterintelligence, expanding and diversifying their legitimate enterprises, and concealing transnational partnerships that could attract undue attention from U.S. intelligence and law enforcement agencies.

POLYDRUG TRAFFICKING ORGANIZATIONS

Mexican polydrug trafficking organizations smuggle large amounts of marijuana, Mexican heroin, cocaine, methamphetamine, and amphetamine into the United States. Law enforcement and intelligence community sources estimate that 65 percent of the cocaine shipped to the United States moves through the Central America-Mexico corridor, primarily by vessels operating in the eastern Pacific. Colombian traffickers utilize fishing vessels to transport bulk shipments of cocaine from Colombia to the west coast of Mexico and, to a lesser extent, the Yucatan Peninsula. The cocaine is off-loaded to go-fast vessels for the final shipment to the Mexican coast. The loads are subsequently broken down into smaller quantities to be moved across the Southwest border.

Through an extensive organization of associates in the United States, often related through family or regional ties, Mexican organizations control the transportation and distribution of illegal drugs from hub cities along the U.S. southwest border to drug consumption markets throughout the United States. As a result of long-term alliances with Colombian organizations, Mexican organizations increasingly have become organized, specialized, and efficient.

---

[4] Paul Kaihla, "The Technology Secrets of Cocaine Inc.," *Business 2.0*, July 2002.
<http://www.business2.com/articles/mag/0,1640,41206,00.html>

Individual components steadily consolidate power and control over well-defined areas of responsibility and geographic strongholds.

Traffickers operating from Mexico now control wholesale cocaine distribution throughout the western and midwestern United States. In cities such as Chicago, Dallas, Denver, Houston, Los Angeles, Phoenix, San Diego, San Francisco, and Seattle, Mexico-based trafficking groups now control the distribution of multi-ton quantities of cocaine. In the early 1990s, when the organized crime groups from Mexico were expanding their roles as cocaine transporters and wholesale-level distributors, most of their U.S.-based command and control operations were in southern California. Today, Chicago is also a key command and control center for their cocaine operations. Currently, these traffickers control cocaine shipments from the time they are smuggled across the border until they are distributed to markets across the United States.[5]

Mexico's polydrug trafficking organizations are known to collaborate in matters such as drug transportation, manufacturing and storage, money laundering, intelligence and sharing of expertise, and development of protection networks. Corruption and the penetration of Mexican institutions at all levels have been favored tactics for decades. Media accounts, as well as well as official U.S. government sources, indicate that an estimated one million dollars per week may be paid to Mexican federal, state, and local officials to ensure the continuous flow of drugs to gateway cities along the Southwestern border of the United States.

The Arellano-Felix Organization

Since the mid-1980s, the Arellano-Felix Organization (AFO) has been one of the most powerful and aggressive drug trafficking networks in Mexico. From strongholds in Tijuana and Mexicali, the AFO orchestrates the transportation, importation, and distribution of multi-ton quantities of cocaine and marijuana and large quantities of heroin and methamphetamine into the United States.

During the mid-1990s, the AFO converted Tijuana into a territory open to the use of various Mexican drug cartels. According to the Mexico City newspaper La Crónica, the AFO

---

[5] Statement by Donnie R. Marshall, Administrator, Drug Enforcement Administration, before the U.S. House of Representatives, Committee on the Judiciary, Subcommittee on Crime, 29 March 2001.
<http://www.usdoj.gov/dea/pubs/cngrtest/ct032901.htm>

established a fee-based system that permitted criminal groups from Chihuahua, Sinaloa, Colima, Tamaulipas, Nayarit, Michoacán and Oaxaca to operate on the Baja California border. According an unnamed Mexican police official, the AFO charged 60 percent of the value of a 500 kilogram or greater shipment of marijuana to organizations that wanted to use Arellano territory to ship drugs into the United States. The AFO's system of "tolls" became a source of violent gang warfare during the latter 1990s when several emerging drug trafficking networks, including the Zambada organization, refused to pay the AFO's fees.[6]

Beyond Mexico, the AFO extended its sphere of influence into source countries in South America such as Colombia and Peru, as well as into trans-shipment countries throughout Central America. The AFO has also developed ties to Russian organized crime and to the Revolutionary Armed Forces of Colombia (Fuerzas Armadas Revolucionarias de Colombia—FARC) terrorist organization.[7]

Violence, intimidation, and corruption have been the AFO's trademarks. Utilizing these "tools of the trade," the AFO developed an internal security apparatus to ensure not only the loyalty of fellow AFO members, but also to ensure compliance by non-AFO traffickers operating in the Baja California corridor. The AFO has been linked to hundreds of murders of informants, Mexican law enforcement officials, rival drug traffickers and innocent citizens. The AFO's aggression has also crossed over the border into the United States.

The AFO suffered serious setbacks during 2002 as a result of stepped up enforcement on both sides of the U.S. border and opportunistic attacks by rival drug trafficking networks. In February and March, the AFO's was dealt two huge blows: the murder of its notorious and brutal enforcer, Ramón Arellano-Felix on February 10, 2002, and the arrest of its overall chief of operations, Benjamin Arellano-Felix, on March 9, 2002. In addition to these losses in the AFO's core organization, Mexican Attorney General Rafael Macedo de la Concha claimed in June 2002 that more than 2,000 AFO-affiliated personnel had been arrested over an 18-month period.[8]

Following the loss of its two top leaders, as well as many mid-level and rank-and-file operatives, the AFO's surviving core leadership faces a severe test of its ability to maintain control over the Tijuana drug corridor, its U.S.-based distribution network, and its transnational

---

[6] Will Weissert, "Mexico's Drug Trade Reorganizes," *Associated Press*, 4 August 2002.
[7] "Colombians Held in Drug Raid," *Orlando Sentinel*, 14 August 2002, A17.
[8] Alfredo Joyner, "El cartel de Tijuana sigue vivo" [The Tijuana Cartel Stays Alive], *Milenio* [Mexico City], 12 June 2002.

supplier and money laundering networks. Day-to-day leadership is widely believed to have devolved to a trio of surviving Arellano Felix siblings led by Francisco Javier Arellano-Felix, alias El Tigrillo (the Little Tiger). His brother, Eduardo, a physician, and his sister Enedina, an accountant, assist the college-educated Javier. This "new generation" of AFO leaders is expected to lead the organization through a period of retrenchment and reorganization that observers predict is likely to produce a smaller scale, as well as a "less violent and more intelligent," criminal drug enterprise.[9]

The Carrillo Fuentes Organization

The Carrillo-Fuentes Organization (CFO), or Juárez Cartel, has eclipsed both the AFO and the Gulf cartel [see below] as the most powerful and geographically extensive Mexico-based polydrug trafficking organization. Despite the death of its leader, Amado Carrillo-Fuentes, in July 1997, the CFO has been able to expand its influence in drug smuggling operations throughout Mexico and the United States. According to media accounts of an intelligence report prepared by the Special Unit Against Organized Crime (Unidad Especializada en Delincuencia Organizada—UEDO), a branch of the Mexican Attorney General's Office, the CFO employs approximately 3,300 persons in as many as 400 cells distributed across 17 Mexican states. The report's findings suggest that the CFO may be the most resilient of the three largest Mexican drug trafficking networks; it has a core leadership of six individuals and a money laundering network headed by 26 regional managers located throughout Mexico.[10]

Vicente Carrillo-Fuentes, brother of Amado, currently oversees cartel operations, in association with a coalition of regional drug barons who were loyal to the cartel before Amado's death. Recent media reports indicate that one of these regional barons, Ismael Zambada García, alias El Mayo, has been aggressively expanding the CFO's territory at the expense of the embattled Arellano-Felix organization and was the author of the February 2002 murder of Ramón Arellano Felix. Another CFO leader, Juan José "El Azul" Esparragoza, has reportedly become an important organization head in his own right, with independent connections to Peruvian and Colombian cocaine suppliers. Esparragoza, who is considered a top advisor to

---

[9] Will Weissert, "Mexico: Bloodlines Long for Mexican Drug Ring," *Arizona Daily Star*, 5 August 2002; and J. Jesús Blancornelas, "Los nuevos Arellano Félix son menos violentos y más de negocios" [The New Arellano Félixes Are Less Violent and More Businesslike], *Crónica* [Mexico City], 1 February 2003.
[10] "'Cartel' de Juarez," *El Universal* [Mexico City], 22 October 2002.

Carillo Fuentes, has been key figure in efforts to settle disputes among the major cartels and has sought to minimizing violence in order to lower the profile of Mexico's drug trafficking networks.[11]

Vicente Carrillo-Fuentes is wanted in Mexico and is also wanted in the United States in connection with a 46-count indictment on charges that include importation and distribution of thousands of kilograms of cocaine and marijuana, murder in furtherance of a continuing criminal enterprise, and ordering the intentional killing of individuals to prevent communication of information to United States law enforcement officers.[12]

The CFO has historically maintained a strong presence in north-central Mexico, including in the cities of Ciudad Juárez and Reynosa. The proximity of these CFO strongholds to the United States allows the CFO command structure to maintain a "hands on" approach in conducting cross border operations. Lower-echelon members travel back and forth between Mexico and the United States, while the leaders rarely venture outside of Mexico. The CFO smuggles tons of cocaine, heroin and marijuana annually to the United States. The CFO's network of cells comprises a transportation and distribution network that spans U.S. cities such as Los Angeles, Houston, Chicago and New York.   In October 2000, the *Washington Times* reported that the CFO had offered a US$200,000 reward for the murder of Drug Enforcement Administration (DEA) agents south of the U.S.-Mexico border. According to the *Times*, the threat was outlined in a confidential FBI memo, warning that "an open contract" had been issued by the CFO for the murder of "U.S. law enforcement officials operating within the Republic of Mexico."[13]

The Cárdenas Guillén Organization

Along with the Arellano Félix (AFO) and Carillo Fuentes (CFO) organizations, the Cárdenas Guillén organization (CGO) has been one of the three enduring pillars of the Mexican polydrug trafficking scene. The CGO is headquartered in the northern states of Tamaulipas and Nuevo León. It has a presence in ten Mexican states, and accounts for approximately 15 percent

---

[11] Will Weissert, "Mexico's Drug Trade Reorganizes," *Hartford Courant*, 5 August 2002.
[12] FBI Wanted Fugitives, September 2002. <http://www.fbi.gov/mostwant/fugitive/sept2002/septfuentes.htm>
[13] Jerry Seper, "Mexican Gang Puts Out Contract on U.S. Narcotics Agent," *Washington Times*, 26 October 2000, A3.

of the cocaine trafficked into the United States through Mexico.[14] According to reports citing the office of Mexico's attorney general, the CGO moves drugs into the United States through Texas and delivers them as far north as New York and Michigan.

As a result of aggressive enforcement by Mexican federal authorities, the CGO has undergone several cycles of core leadership loss and replacement since its co-founder, Juan García Abrego, was extradited to the United States in 1997. New leaders, including current head Osiel Cárdenas Guillén, have emerged from among a loose coalition of regional drug barons who trace their origins to the Matamoros-based trafficking network created by García Abrego and Juan N. Guerra during the 1980s.

Recent local newspaper accounts and a Mexican government report indicate that, during 2001, the CGO split into at least two factions, one led by Osiel Cárdenas Guillén and another led by Baudelio López Falcón, alias El Yeyo. The Cardenas Guillén faction, based in the cities of Matamoros, Reynosa, and Ciudad Miguel Alemán, has attempted a violent takeover of López Falcón strongholds in the states of Nuevo León and in the border city of Nuevo Laredo. The escalating dispute led to dozens of gangland style killings in Nuevo Laredo and Monterrey during 2002, and prompted the deployment of more than 500 Mexican federal troops to the area during the fall.[15] Cardenas Guillén's bid to expand his territory into Nuevo León, which until now has served as a neutral "buffer zone" between the major trafficking groups, also appears have upset a delicate truce between Cárdenas Guillén and the Carillo Fuentes family.[16]

One local newspaper account has raised doubts about Guillén's leadership status within the CGO. Citing a confidential Secretariat of National Defense report, the story in Monterrey's *El Norte* newspaper claims that the high-profile Guillén may in fact be an enforcer and manager for Julio César Longoria Narváez, alias Ramiro Longoria, a prominent businessman from Tamaulipas state who has been previously linked to cocaine trafficking and official bribery.[17]

---

[14] Procuraduría General de la República, *Programa Nacional para el Control de Drogas: 2001-2006* [Mexico City], 2002, 59. <http://www.pgr.gob.mx>

[15] Karen Brooks, "Authorities Gather to Combat Warring Drug Cartels," *Chicago Tribune*, 4 October 2002.

[16] Mario Alvarez, "Disputan dos carteles plaza de Nuevo León" [Two Cartels Dispute the Nuevo León Drug Corridor], *Reforma* [Mexico City], 8 September 2002, 2.

[17] Martin Morita, "Descartan a Osiel Como Lider de Cartel" [Osiel's Cartel Leadership Downplayed], *El Norte*, Monterrey, Mexico, 3 April 2002, 2.

The Zambada García Organization

This Zambada organization, led by Ismael "El Mayo" Zambada García, has operated for almost three decades as a mid-sized drug smuggling group based in Mazatlán, in the western state of Sinaloa.[18] A former farmer with extensive agricultural and botanical knowledge, the 53-year-old Zambada has worked in recent years to increase his gang's production of heroin while consolidating his position as a trafficker of Colombian cocaine. Known as an accomplished alliance builder, Zambada has historically worked closely with the Juárez cartel and the Carillo Fuentes family while maintaining independent ties to Colombian cocaine suppliers. Several news accounts have described Zambada as an upwardly mobile enforcer for the Juárez cartel who gained in stature after the death of Amado Carrillo Fuentes. According to a U.S. law enforcement official quoted in the *Los Angeles Times*, Zambada "learned early on how to hitch his wagon to other bigger organizations, and this has given him entree."[19] Zambada is said to have been a former Arellano-Felix ally before a disagreement over drug payments broke out into a gang war between Zambada and the AFO's enforcer, Ramón Arellano-Felix. The latter was killed in a February 2002 shootout in Zambada's home city of Mazatlán by local police widely believed to have been on Zambada's payroll.

In the wake of the disruption to the AFO caused by the death of Ramón Arellano-Felix and the capture of his bother, Benjamín, Zambada has intensified his efforts to gain control of AFO operations in the states of Sinaloa, Jalisco, and Michoacán.[20] Zambada's bid for the AFO's territory has led to a violent gang war between factions loyal to AFO heir Francisco Javier Arellano-Felix, alias El Tigrillo, and breakaway groups aligned with Zambada. The latter has also been described as a suspect in the February 2000 murder of Tijuana police chief Alfredo de la Torre. Although he is openly hostile to the AFO, Zambada has an informal non-aggression pact with Joaquin "El Chapo" Guzmán Loera, who controls another Sinaloa-based drug gang (see Guzmán Loera/Palma Salazar Organization).[21] Mexican print media have reported that Zambada's inlaws, based in the city of Valladolid, in Yucatán state, have expanded his drug

---

[18] "Three Groups Vying to Take Over Drug Trade in Baja California," *The News: Mexico* [Mexico City], 26 March 2002.

[19] Chris Kaul, "Coastal Drug Kingpin Eyes Tijuana Turf," *Los Angeles Times*, 19 March 2002.

[20] Lenny Savino and Kevin G. Hall, "War Over Dead Brothers' Mexican Drug Cartel Heating Up," *Chicago Tribune-Knight Ridder News Service*, 31 March 2002, 1.

[21] Will Weissert, "Mexico's Drug Trade Reorganizes," Associated Press/*Hartford Courant*, 5 August 2002.

trafficking enterprise into the Yucatán peninsula.[22] In addition to Sinaloa, Yucatán, Jalisco, and Michoacán, Zambada Organization cells have also been identified in the gulf coast states of Campeche, Quintana Roo, and Tabasco.

Zambada has been wanted by Mexico's attorney general's office since 1998, when it issued bounties totaling US$2.8 million on him and five other leaders of the Juárez cartel. In recognition of the emerging threat posed by the Zambada drug trafficking organization, in May 2002 the Bush Administration designated Zambada a drug kingpin eligible for sanctions pursuant to the Foreign Narcotics Kingpin Designation Act.[23]

The Amezcua-Contreras Organization

The Amezcua-Contreras family manages a synthetic drug production and trafficking organization with global dimensions. The organization, also known as the Colima cartel, specializes in the production of methamphetamine and "ecstasy" and directly handles their smuggling into the United States. It is based in the western cities of Guadalajara and Colima and has a presence in eight Mexican states.

The organization began in 1988 as an alien smuggling ring.[24] It subsequently shifted the focus of its operations to cocaine and methamphetamine trafficking. During the early 1990s (the height of the organization's existence), the Amezcua organization was considered one of the world's largest smugglers of ephedrine and clandestine producers of methamphetamine. The Amezcua-Contreras brothers obtained large quantities of the precursor ephedrine, utilizing contacts in Thailand and India, which they supplied to methamphetamine laboratories in Mexico and southern California.[25] The Amezcua organization has also been known to supply methamphetamine to the Arellano-Felix organization, and has trafficked in cocaine in association with Colombia's Cali cartel.

---

[22] "Lidera 'El Mayo' Cédula en Yucatán" ['El Mayo' Leads Cell in Yucatán], *Frontera./EFE*, [Tijuana], 5 October 2002. <http://www.frontera.info/notasenlinea/noticias/20021005/11439.asp>

[23] U.S. Department of State, "Fact Sheet: Drug Traffickers Targeted by U.S. Kingpin Act," 31 May 2002. <http://usinfo.state.gov/topical/global/drugs/02053104.htm>

[24] Isaac Guzman, "De polleros as reyes del narco" [From Alien Smugglers to Kingpins], *Reforma* [Mexico City], 3 June 2001, 12.

[25] Statement by Thomas A. Constantine, Drug Enforcement Administration, United States Department of Justice, before the U.S. House of Representatives, Subcommittee on Criminal Justice, Drug Policy and Human Resources, 4 March 1999. < http://www.usdoj.gov/dea/pubs/cngrtest/ct030499.htm >

In May 2001, Adán Amezcua was arrested in Mexico on money laundering charges. He joined his two older brothers, Luis and Jose de Jesus Amezcua, who are serving prison sentences in Mexico on narcotics-related charges. In May 2002, a Mexican federal court blocked the scheduled extradition of José de Jesús Amezcua to the United States to face drug trafficking charges because the U.S. extradition request did not comply with Mexico's requirement that extradited criminals not face the possibility of capital punishment or a life sentence.[26] Day-to-day management of the organization is believed to have passed to two sisters of the Amezcua-Contreras clan who remain at large. It is likely that the male family members also continue to be involved in running the organization from prison.

The Caro-Quintero Organization

The Caro-Quintero Organization (CQO) cultivates cannabis throughout Mexico, and smuggles marijuana, heroin and cocaine from Mexico into the United States. Miguel Angel Caro-Quintero became the head of the Caro-Quintero organization after the 1985 imprisonment of his brother, Rafael Caro-Quintero, on drug violations and his involvement in the murder of DEA Special Agent Enrique Camarena. After a prolonged manhunt by Mexican federal police, Miguel Caro Quintero was arrested in December 2001 in Sinaloa. In addition to facing drug trafficking charges in Mexico, he is sought by U.S. authorities based on two federal indictments in Arizona and two in Colorado.[27] During 2002 the Mexican Secretariat of Foreign Affairs sought to honor the U.S. extradition request of Caro Quintero but was thwarted by appeals filed by CQO attorneys.[28]

The CQO is based in the town of Caborca, in the northern state of Sonora, as well as in the state capitol of Hermosillo. The remnants of CQO operations are expected to be passed along to Miguel Caro-Quintero's brothers, Jorge and Genaro Caro-Quintero, and his sisters Maria Del Carmen Caro-Quintero, Blanca Lili Caro-Quintero, Melida Caro de Arce, and Maria Manuela Caro de Sesteaga.[29]

---

[26] Abel Barajas, "Rechazan extraditar a Amezcua" [Amezcua Extradition Rejected], *El Norte* [Monterrey, Mexico], 22 May 2002.
[27] "Extradition of Alleged Drug Figure Approved," *San Diego Union-Tribune*, 28 November 2002, A23.
[28] Abel Barajas, "Para Extradición de Caro Quintero" [Caro Quintero Extradition Halted], *Reforma* [Mexico City], 20 December 2002. <http://www.reforma.com/nacional/articulo/255317/>
[29] Statement by Thomas A. Constantine.

The Guzmán/Palma Organization

This drug trafficking organization, based in the states of Sinaloa and Jalisco, has been degraded in recent years as a result of a violent gang war with the stronger Arellano-Felix organization. However, it appears that aggressive enforcement against the Tijuana cartel since 2001 may have given the Sinaloa/Jaliso cartel an opportunity to recover. Despite the setbacks of recent years, including the arrest of two of its top kingpins, the Sinaloa/Jalisco cartel continues to maintain a presence in twelve Mexican states. In a display of its continuing ability to corrupt public officials, cartel leader Joaquín "El Chapo" Guzmán Loera escaped from a Mexican prison in January 2000 with the assistance of prison guards. Guzmán was serving a 40-year sentence for narcotics trafficking. Despite the Fox administration's announcement that the recapture of "El Chapo" Guzmán is a top anti-narcotics enforcement priority, the fugitive drug boss remains at large at the time of this writing.

Another organization leader, Hector Luis "El Güero" Palma Salazar, also attempted a prison escape in December 2002 after he was transferred out of the maximum-security wing of his prison by order of a Mexican judge.[30] Palma Salazar's unsuccessful escape attempt appears to have been prompted by news that he was eligible to be extradited to the United States to face drug trafficking charges. The Sinalo/Jalisco cartel has historically cooperated with the Carillo-Fuentes organization. Carillo-Fuentes adviser Juan "El Azul" Esparragoza is also believed to play an important role in the Sinaloa/Jalisco organization.[31]

The Espinoza Ramírez Organization

This organization, headed by the Colombian trafficker Juan Diego Espinoza Ramírez, alias El Tigre, and his brother, Mauricio, specializes in the transportion of multi-ton quantities of Colombian cocaine through Mexico into the United States. The Espinoza Ramírez organization maintains a cooperative relationship with the Carillo Fuentes, Guzman Loera, and Zambada García organizations. All four organizations are suspected of having shared information obtained from the "informant network" within the Mexican government that was uncovered in October

---

[30] "Frustran intento de fuga de *El Guero* Palma" [*El Guero* Palma Escape Attempt Foiled], *Milenio* [Mexico City], 18 December 2002.
[31] Mike Gallagher, "King of the Kingpins," *Albuquerque Journal*, 3 March 1997, A1.

2002.[32] Espinoza's criminal enterprise operates in the state of Sonora as well as in Mexico City and Cancún.

Mexican authorities have linked the Espinoza organization to the *Macel*, a drug-laden ship carrying 9.2 tons of cocaine that the Mexican Navy intercepted in December 2001.[33] Mexico's police agencies began a major investigation into the Espinoza drug network in July 2002, when authorities questioning two Colombian women accused of smuggling $US2.4 million through the Mexico City airport discovered their ties to Espinoza.[34]

In October 2002, Mexican authorities reportedly seized more than 200 vehicles and properties belonging to Espinoza. According to the Mexican Attorney General's office (PGR) the properties, worth some $US2.1 million, were seized in Hermosillo, Sonora, and were legally registered in the name of Espinoza Ramírez' wife, Sandra Avila Beltrán.[35]

The Valencia Organization

This drug trafficking organization, also known as the Millenium cartel (cartel del Milenio), is based in Guadalajara, Jalisco, and the state of Michoacán. The DEA has identified cartel bosses Armando Valencia-Cornelio and Luis Valencia Valencia as key figures in the interrelationship between major Mexican and Colombian drug trafficking organizations.[36] The DEA estimates that the AVO has received up to 20 tons of cocaine a month for resale and distribution to Mexican drug trafficking networks. These shipments are transported primarily to the west coast of Mexico from the north coast of Colombia via maritime vessel and are ultimately moved north for smuggling into the United States.

The Díaz Parada Organization

This organization, led by Pedro Díaz Parada, is based in the southwestern state of Oaxaca. According to the Mexican Attorney General's office, Díaz Parada organization cells have been detected in seven Mexican states, including Veracruz, Chiapas, Durango, and

---

[32] Ivan Frutos, "Resaltan la influencia del narco en Sinaloa" [Narcotraffickers' Influence in Sinaloa Grows], *El Norte* [Monterrey, Mexico], 24 October 2002, 5.

[33] "Decomisa PGR bienes de presuntos narcotraficantes," *El Norte* [Monterrey, Mexico], 7 October 2002, 2.

[34] "Detienen narcos ligados a El Tigre," *El Norte* [Monterrey, Mexico], 21 October 2002, 13.

[35] *El Norte*, 7 October 2002.

[36] United States Drug Enforcement Administration. *Drug Intelligence Brief: Mexico Country Brief*, July 2002. <http://www.usdoj.gov/dea/pubs/intel/02035/02035p.html>

Chihuahua. Díaz Parada is a fugitive who escaped from a Oaxacan prison in 1985 after being sentenced on drug trafficking charges. In 1987, a Diaz Parada lieutenant murdered the federal judge who had sentenced the drug kingpin in 1985.[37] Diaz Parada's organization is believed to cooperate with the Arellano-Felix organization and is considered one of the seven largest drug trafficking networks in Mexico.

The Eduviko García Organization

In the spring of 2001, the DEA publicly revealed the existence of this organization, which specializes in smuggling methamphetamine into the United States through the Nuevo Laredo-Laredo border area.[38] This new organization is headquartered in Nuevo Laredo and is headed by Eduviko García. According to DEA congressional testimony, García received methamphetamine through a Nuevo Laredo, Mexico-based facilitator who in turn received methamphetamine from a variety of Mexican based sources.[39] Methamphetamine seized in the García investigation has been tied to Francisco Zarragoza, a methamphetamine source based in Guadalajara. The DEA's investigation of García in 2001 resulted in the seizure of 53 pounds of methamphetamine, 18 kilograms of cocaine, and the arrest of 50 individuals.

The "MaBaker" Buendía Organization

This drug trafficking organization, based in the Mexico City suburb of Ciudad Nezahualcóyotle (Ciudad Neza), primarily traffics in cocaine destined for the domestic urban market. It was until recently led by Delia Patricia Buendía, alias Ma Baker, and Carlos Morales Correa, alias El Aguila. The Buendía gang, which is known to have ties to the three major Mexican cartels, disposes of "surplus" cocaine belonging to the cartels by selling it in the local Mexico City street market. According to one local newspaper account, the Buendía gang's operations expanded significantly after tightened border security measures in the wake of the September 11 attacks on the United States left the major drug cartels with large amounts of

---

[37] "Salió libre narcotraficante acusado de matar a Juez Federal" [Narcotrafficker Accused of Murdering Federal Judge Set Free], *La Unión de Morelos* [Cuernavaca, Mexico], 4 June 2002.

[38] "Detecta DEA banda de droga sintética" [DEA Detects Synthetic Drug Gang], *Reforma* [Mexico City], 17 August 2001.

[39] Statement by Errol J. Chavez, Special Agent in Charge, San Diego Field Division Drug Enforcement Administration, before the U.S. House of Representatives, Committee on Government Reform, Subcommittee on Government Efficiency, Financial Management, and Intergovernmental Relations, 13 April 2001. <http://www.usdoj.gov/dea/pubs/cngrtest/ct041301.htm>

cocaine that could not be easily shipped north.[40] The Buendía organization is known to have penetrated elements of the Mexico City police force.[41] The organization is believed to have carried out the assassinations of several policemen, including federal police commander Guillermo Robles Liceaga. In August 2002, Mexican federal police arrested Delia Buendía, Carlos Morales, and four other Neza cartel leaders.

The Herrera Family Organization

Recent and historical intelligence has identified the Herrera family as one of the larger Mexican organizations specializing in heroin production and trafficking.[42] The scope of the Herrera family's illicit enterprise reaches distribution networks in the United States, and their influence in the Mexican heroin trafficking culture is considerable. The Herrera organization, based in Durango, Mexico, historically was judged to be the most notorious heroin trafficking group in Mexico, and has been in operation since the mid-1950s.[43] The organization is reported to comprise multiple families, all of which are related to the Herrera family through either blood or marriage. The patriarch of the Herrera family, Jaime Herrera-Nevarez, was arrested in Guadalajara, Mexico in 1987. In addition to trafficking heroin, it was reported that the Herrera organization has expanded its operations to include trafficking in large quantities of cocaine. The organization also is reported to traffic, albeit to a lesser extent, marijuana and methamphetamine.

The Herrera organization commonly uses vehicles to transport its drugs. Drugs are concealed in hidden compartments located within the transport vehicle, which is driven from Mexico through El Paso, Texas, and then on to Chicago, Illinois. The Herreras also have used tractor-trailers to transport large quantities of drugs, such as cocaine, concealed in loads of legitimate goods. Intelligence gathered from two recent heroin laboratory seizures that occurred in the state of Durango indicates that the members of the Herrera family continue to be active in the Mexican heroin trade.

---

[40] Ignacio Alzaga, "Atentados en EU fortalecieron operaciones del cartel de Neza [Attacks on the U.S. Srengthened Neza Cartel Operations], *El Sol de Mexico* [Mexico City], 30 August 2002.

[41] Ioan Grillo, "PGR Investigation into Drug Network to Lead to Crackdown on Police Corruption," *The News: Mexico*, 22 August 2002.

[42] U.S. Drug Enforcement Administration "The Mexican Heroin Trade," April 2000 (DEA-20014). <http://www.usdoj.gov/dea/pubs/intel/20014/20014.html>

[43] Molly Moore and Douglas Farah, "Mexican Heroin on Rise in U.S.," *Washington Post*, 2 June 1998, A1.

NORTHERN BORDER SMUGGLING GANGS

The Herrera/Rubio "Los Texas" Gang

This border gang is based in the northern states of Coahuila and Tamaulipas and maintains cells in San Antonio and Laredo, Texas. The Los Texas is known to engage in drug trafficking, kidnapping, and violent enforcement in association with the Arellano-Felix organization, and may also be participating in alien smuggling. Arturo Martínez Herrera, alias El Texas, heads the gang. Herrera has been serving a 36-year sentence for drug trafficking since 1994, but is believed to exercise some command and control over the Los Texas gang from prison. During 2001, Herrera engaged in unsuccessful legal maneuvers to secure an early release.[44] The gang is one of several that are active in the Piedras Negras-Eagle Pass and Nuevo Laredo-Laredo border zones. Members of Los Texas have been linked to dozens of gangland style murders over the past several years. Los Texas maintains a longstanding rivalry with "Los Chachos," another northern border gang that is linked to the Gulf cartel. At least one Los Texas leader, Omar Rubio Fayette, alias El Vampiro, is wanted by the DEA for conspiracy to distribute marijuana.[45] As of this writing, Rubio Fayette remains at large.

The Román García "Los Chachos" Gang

The "Los Chachos" gang began as a cross-border automobile theft ring and later turned to drug smuggling. It is based in the northern cities of Anáhuac, Monterrey, and Reynosa.[46] Los Chachos, which is believed to have 50 to 60 core members, was originally associated with the Gulf cartel under the leadership of Juan García Abrego. In recent years, however, the group appears to have realigned itself with the Arellano Félix organization. In May 2002, the organization's leader, Dionisio Román García, alias El Chacho, and his top lieutenant, Juvenal Torres Sánchez, were assassinated in Monterrey. According to Mexican law enforcement sources, El Chacho's murder appears to have been carried out by the Cardenas Guillén wing of the Gulf cartel. In October, the Mexican Attorney General's Office reported that the Los

---

[44] Victor Fuentes, "Pide capo absolución a la corte" [Kingpin Seeks Pardon from Court], *El Norte* [Monterrey, Mexico], 21 August 2001.
[45] United States Drug Enforcement Administration, *DEA Briefs: Dallas Field Division Wanted List.* <http://www.usdoj.gov/dea/fugitives/dallas/rubio.htm>
[46] Martha Cazares, "El Chacho: De ladrón de autos a capo de la frontera" [El Chacho: From Car Thief to Border Kingpin], *El Norte* [Monterrey: Mexico], 16 May 2002, 11.

Chachos gang was reorganizing under the command of three surviving Román García lieutenants: José Angel Fernández, Raúl Emmanuel Cárdenas Castillo, and Edgar Valdés Villareal.[47]

The Jesús Lugo "Los Sinaloa" Gang

The "Los Sinaloa" border drug smuggling gang is based in the northern state of Chihuahua and has historically been affiliated with the Juárez cartel. The gang specializes in transporting cocaine northward through Mexico toward and across the U.S. border. In December 2001, a Cessna aircraft specially fitted to transport drugs and possibly belonging to the group was found abandoned on the runway at the airport in Piedras Negras, Coahuila.[48] The group's founder, Jesús Lugo "El Chuy Sinaloa" is a native of the town of Navolato in the state of Sinaloa and was a lieutenant of Amado Carillo Fuentes.[49] The Los Sinaloa gang is notorious for its extreme violence and its ready access to large-caliber automatic weapons, including AK-47 assault rifles. The gang is blamed for an August 2001 massacre in the town of Madera in western Chihuahua that left seven people dead and two seriously injured. Mexican media accounts portray the gang as having enjoyed blanket protection from local law enforcement until the August 2001 massacre, when federal authorities initiated a manhunt for the shooters. Two weeks after the massacre, four commanders of the state judicial police were removed from their posts for allegedly cooperating with drug traffickers.[50]

The "Los Michoacanos" Gang

The "Los Michoacanos" border drug smuggling gang is active in the state of Coahuila. Members of the gang have been spotted in the Boquillas-Big Bend National Park area as well as

---

[47] Hecto Castro, Luis García, and Luis Antonio Rivera, "Busca PGR en NL a 'Los Cachos'" [PGR Seeks Los Chachos in Nuevo León], *El Norte* [Monterrey: Mexico], 15 October 2002.

[48] Francisco Linan, "Frenan en Piedras Negras el caso de narcoavioneta" [The Narco-Plane Case in Piedras Negras Stalls], El Norte [Monterrey, Mexico], 2 December 2002, 19.

[49] Enrique Lomas, "Caen dos de 'Los Sinaloa'" [Two Members of 'Los Sinaloa' Captured], *El Norte* [Monterrey: Mexico], 17 August 2001, 17.

[50] Enrique Lomas, "Cesan en Chihuahua a cuatro comandantes," [Four Chihuahua Commanders Dismissed], *El Norte*, [Monterrey: Mexico], 30 August 2001, 15.

in the border town of Piedras Negras, across from Eagle Pass. According to Mexican newspaper accounts, the gang has historically operated as a cell of the Juárez cartel.[51]

The "Los Tres de la Sierra" Gang

During the late 1990s, this border drug gang, based in the state of Chihuahua, controlled a large portion of the U.S.-bound drug flow in the Ojinaga-Presidio area, along Route 67 near Big Bend National Park. The group's name, which means "the three from the mountains," refers to the gang's three top bosses: Francisco "Kiko" Balderrama-Rios, Armando Quiróz-García, and Rubén Carrasco-Valdéz. The three men were named in a 24-count U.S. federal indictment in which they were charged with running a Continuing Criminal Enterprise (CCE) that imported and distributed over 62 tons of marijuana into the United States.[52] In late September 2000, Balderrama and Quiróz were apprehended in Sydney, Australia, and Carrasco was captured in Hawaii. All three men had traveled to Australia to watch the Olympic games. Balderrama and Quiróz briefly escaped from prison in Sydney but were recaptured and extradited to the United States in June 2002.[53]

The "Los Tigres de Guerrero" Gang

The "Los Tres de Guerrero" drug gang, which operates in the Nuevo Laredo and Piedras Negras areas, has been linked to arms smuggling as well as marijuana and heroin trafficking. In June 2000, Mexican federal police captured six members of the group who were found to be in possession of several high-powered firearms—including a rifle grenade—as well as three kilograms of marijuana.[54] The group was mentioned in a June 2002 newspaper account as one of several drug gangs that continue to be active in the Piedras Negras area.[55]

---

[51] Efrain Klerigan, "Big Bend Abriga a narcos e ilegales" [Big Bend Harbors Drug Traffickers and Illegals], *El Norte* [Monterrey:Mexico], 30 October 2000, 20.

[52] U.S. Attorney's Office, Western District of Texas, Press Release, "Australians and Americans Share Gold Medal in Apprehending International Drug Dealers," 29 September 2002. <http://www.usdoj.gov/usao/txw/Balderrama.htm>

[53] United States Drug Enforcement Administration, News Release, "Two Drug Smugglers Are Extradited to Alpine, Texas," 4 June 2002. <http://www.usdoj.gov/dea/pubs/states/newsrel/texas060402p.html>

[54] "Caen 6 de la banda 'Los Tigres de Guerrero'" [Six Members of 'Los Tigres de Guerrero' Captured], Reforma [Mexico City], 21 June 2000, 18.

[55] Francisco Linan, "Realiza Procuraduría cateos a agents en Piedras Negras" [Attorney General Investigates Police in Piedras Negras], *Reforma* [Mexico City], 1 June 2002, 16.

ALIEN SMUGGLING NETWORKS

Alien smuggling from Mexico to the United States is a US$300 million-a-year business, second only to Mexico's illicit drug trade in terms of revenues from criminal activities.[56] The criminal organizations involved in alien smuggling through Mexico are highly efficient movers of people across national frontiers. Unlike other international criminal organizations, some of which smuggle illegal aliens as an adjunct to other criminal activities, alien smuggling groups typically are less hierarchical and more characterized by loose networks of associates to facilitate the movement of illegal migrants across regions and continents. These networks typically include local agents who recruit people interested in illegal immigration to the United States and elsewhere and bring them together for departure; travel processors who arrange for identification and any necessary travel documents; and international "brokers" along the way who facilitate intermediate passages and make arrangements for arrival at final destinations. The widespread dispersion of associates gives alien smuggling groups the flexibility to quickly and easily shift routes or call upon different operatives if law enforcement or other conditions disrupt their operations. The fact that groups of illegal aliens are typically handed from smuggler to smuggler during portions of their journey makes it difficult to target and disrupt alien smuggling networks. Mexico's alien smuggling networks include an abundance of smugglers and escorts, fraudulent document vendors, safehouse keepers, corrupt airline and bus company employees, and corrupt officials. Although many alien smuggling groups are highly specialized, the growing profitability of this criminal business has increased the involvement of larger polycrime syndicates. Some groups have engaged in moving both drugs and people, although not necessarily at the same time.

Exactly how many alien smuggling organizations are operating in Mexico is unknown, but the number is believed to be substantial. According to an INS intelligence report cited in a recent General Accounting Office (GAO) report, various sources have estimated that there may be up to 300 alien smuggling rings in Mexico.[57] Mexican media have widely cited a report by Mexico's intelligence service that claims there are about 100 Mexican alien smuggling rings

---

[56] "Study Says Mexico Migrant Traffic Is a $300 Million a Year Trade," *Reuters*, 14 June 2001. <http://www.usbc.org/info/crime/0601trade.htm>
[57] United States, General Accounting Office, *Alien Smuggling: Management and Operational Improvements Needed to Address Growing Problem* (Report GAO/GGD-00-103), 1 May 2000.

linked to half a dozen core networks.[58] The core networks are believed to have operatives throughout the Central American isthmus as well as in parts of South America. Some of the larger networks are also believed to have partnerships with East Asian alien smuggling groups and possibly Russian or Ukrainian organized crime groups.

The core smuggling networks communicate around the globe. They rely on cell phones with hard-to-trace numbers as well as on more sophisticated digital equipment. Along the U.S.-Mexico border, smugglers possess the technology to observe, and then communicate to their field operatives the shifting deployments of the Border Patrol and its monitoring equipment. This capability has set off a technological arms race. As the Border Patrol pours more resources into night-vision scopes, weight sensors, and giant X-ray machines for seeing into trucks, smuggling rings counter with their own state-of-the-art equipment paid for by increased fees. Smuggling operations such as the Peralta organization (see Peralta-Rodríguez Organization below) are capable of gathering individuals from all over the world and transporting them north across the border and on to distant U.S. cities. Large ranches in Mexico serve as staging areas where hundreds of immigrants can be housed and fed until ready to be moved north. In the United States, smuggling rings operate networks of drop houses where illegal immigrants are kept until they arrive at their destinations—and until their relatives pay off the balance of their fees.[59]

The Peralta-Rodríguez Organization

Since the early 1980s, the criminal organization run by the Peralta-Rodríguez family has been a significant presence in Mexico's human smuggling trade. During the height of its operations in the late 1990s, the Peralta-Rodríguez organization smuggled up to 1,000 immigrants into the United States per week, charging between $800 and $1,200 per person. A seven-year investigation of the Peralta smuggling network by the FBI revealed that the group was highly sophisticated and employed a substantial network of recruiters, escorts, and drivers, as well as transportation and lodging providers, and document forgery specialists. Assistant U.S. Attorney Michael Skerlos said group members were supplied with high-quality cellular phones and a fleet of vans and cars.[60] They rented houses and paid for hotel rooms throughout Southern

---

[58] Héctor López Cruz, "Autoridades de 23 estados están involucradas en tráfico de ilegales" [Authorities in 23 States Are Involved in Alien Smuggling], *Crónica* [Mexico City], 23 July 2001.

[59] Peter Skerry, "The Cost of a Tighter Border: People Smuggling Networks," *Los Angeles Times*, 3 May 1998, 2.

[60] Office of the United States Attorney, Southern District of California, *Press Release*, 21 June, 2000.

California to provide shelter for the migrants. The ring set up smuggling corridors from Tijuana to San Diego, El Centro, and Los Angeles. In each city, a core of people oversaw the transportation of migrants from their assigned areas. The Peraltas are believed to recruit most of their workers from Salvatierra, a small town in their home state of Guanajuato.

The organization is believed to have invested large sums of money to buy protection from corrupt law enforcement officials along the length of its smuggling routes. Alluding to the organization's scope and resources, Mexican border expert Victor Clark Alfaro has described the Peraltas as "the Arellano-Félix brothers of human smuggling."[61] The organization suffered a major blow in the spring of 2000, when a seven-year investigation of the group led to the arrest of more than 60 operatives in the United States. Despite this setback, the Peralta network continues to function at a reduced level of activity under the leadership of Vicente and José Ismael Peralta, both of whom remained at large in December 2002.

The "Los Tello" Organization

The "Los Tello" alien smuggling ring has been described in Mexican media accounts as a Tijuana-based organization that competes fiercely with the Peralta-Rodríguez family for the U.S. southwest border alien smuggling trade. The group's leader, known only as "El Tello," is a longtime alien smuggler who recruits illegal border crossers at the Municipal Market in Tijuana, near the Tijuana Cathedral. The El Tello ring has been known to smuggle aliens across the U.S. border near the towns of El Hongo (kilometer 98 of the Tijuana-La Rumorosa highway) and La Hechicera (kilometer 71 of the same highway).[62]

The Castillo Organization

This Honduras-based organization is believed to manage one of the largest multinational alien smuggling rings ever conducted in the Western Hemisphere. The Castillo organization specializes in the overland smuggling of Central and South American migrants through Mexico and across the U.S. southwest border. Honduran national José León Castillo, alias Leoncio Castillo, led the organization until his arrest in Guatemala and deportation to the United States in

---

[61] Marisa Taylor, "Immigrant Smuggling Ring Is Dealt a Severe Blow," *San Diego Union-Tribune*, 27 July 2000, B-1.

[62] Jorge Morales, "Revelan operación y centros de tráfico de migrantes" [Migrant Trafficking Operations and Centers Revealed], *Frontera*, 3 January 2001.
<http://www.frontera.info/edicionimpresa/traernota.asp?NumNota=81885>

October 2000. Castillo's network has cells in every Central American country as well as in Mexico, where 12 Castillo operatives were arrested in the fall of 2000 as part of the multi-national Operation Forerunner.[63] During that operation, 3,500 migrants bound for the United States with the assistance of the Castillo ring were intercepted and returned to their countries of origin.[64]

The Martínez Terán Organization

According to a 2001 Federal Preventive Police (PFP) report leaked to the Mexican newsmagazine, *Crónica*, the Martínez Terán organization may be the single largest alien smuggling ring in Mexico. The organization's operations span the entire Western Hemisphere, and it is suspected of having collaborative relationships with Asian human smuggling rings.[65] The organization's kingpin, Carlos Martínez Terán, alias El Yato, has been in Mexican federal custody since January 2000. Terán's wife and mother-in-law were arrested in April 2000 as they escorted 75 undocumented Central Americans who were in transit to the United States through the state of Oaxaca.[66] According to the *Crónica* report, as of mid-2001 Mexican federal police believed several cells of the Martínez Terán ring continued to function under the control of organization lieutenants who remained at large. These lieutenants included: Ángela and Pedro Olivas Álvarez, Felipe and Laura Sánchez Olivas, Jesús Cereceres Tarango, Consuelo Lobato Guitiérrez, Sofía Leanos Lobatos, Francisco Aguilar Méndez, Trinidad Gaspar Gaspar, and Adán Martínez Chacón.

The Castorena-San Germán Organization

This organization, based in Guadalajara, directs a vast network of document forgery rings that distribute falsified documents to Hispanic illegal aliens across the United States. Documents produced by the Castorena-San Germán organization have been discovered in 55 U.S. cities and

---

[63] Maribel Gonzalez, "Cae banda de 'polleros' [Alien Smuggling Ring Captured], *El Norte* [Monterrey, Mexico] 18 October 2000, 2.

[64] Immigration and Naturalization Service Press Release, "INS and Central American Governments Disrupt Alien Smuggling Operations," 17 October 2000.

[65] Héctor López Cruz, "Autoridades de 23 estados están involucradas en tráfco de lilgales" [Authorities in 23 States Are Involved in Alien Smuggling], Crónica, 23 July 2001.

[66] "Inicia Mexico cruzada para desarticular redes de tráfico de personas" [Mexico Launches Effort to Dismantle Human Trafficking Networks], *Notimex* [Mexico City], 2 April 2000.

32 states, according to Los Angeles INS district director Tom Schiltgen.[67] Alfonso Castorena founded the Castorena-San Germán document forgery enterprise. Known respectfully in Guadalajara as "Don Alfonso," Castorena and his associates built a counterfeiting empire in the United States by printing high-quality documents and distributing them with help from street gangs, according to law enforcement officials and court records cited by the *Chicago Tribune*.

Until his arrest in November 1998, Juan San Germán was the Castorena operations chief in the United States. San Germán maintained operations centers in Chicago and Los Angeles, among other U.S. cities. At one point, an eyewitness reported that San Germán had described Chicago as "by far the busiest and most profitable [forged] document center in the nation."[68] In 1998, the U.S. Immigration and Naturalization Service seized 31,000 counterfeit documents in Chicago's Little Village neighborhood that were printed and distributed by the Castorena-San Germán organization with the assistance of the Latin Kings street gang. In Las Vegas and Los Angeles, the 18th Street gang has also been linked to the sale of documents produced by the Castorena-San Germán group.

In November 1998, federal authorities in Los Angeles apprehended Juan San Germán and 10 accomplices. The results of a federal investigation also uncovered approximately 2 million falsified documents belonging to the San Germán organization in a Los Angeles public storage facility.[69] In October 1999, San Germán pled guilty to four felony counts. He was sentenced to six-and-half years in federal prison in January 2000 for his conviction on charges of conspiracy, fraud and misuse of identity documents, possession and transfer of false identity documents, and possession of document-making implements.

The Iglesias Rebollo Organization/Titanium Group

This prostitution and human trafficking ring traffics in women from Central Europe Central America, and South America.[70] Through a network of 16 nightclubs in Mexico City, the Titanium Group operates a criminal enterprise that colludes with foreign organized crime syndicates, possibly the Russian or Ukrainian mafias, to traffic in women from Hungary for

---

[67] Sylvia Pagan Westphal, "Fighting the Fakes," *Los Angeles Times*, 11 February 2000, B-2.
[68] Gary Marx and Teresa Puente, "Fake Papers Net Real Cash: Latin Kings Prey on Need for Illegal Documents," *Chicago Tribune*, 19 September 1999, 1.
[69] United States Attorney, Central District of California, Press Release, "Ringleader of Massive Scheme to Make and Sell False Immigration Documents Sentenced to 6½ Years," 10 January 2000.
<http://www.usdoj.gov/usao/cac/pr/pr2000/009.htm>
[70] "The Lobohombo Case: Drugs and Human Trafficking," *The News* [Mexico City], 11 January 2000.

purposes of sexual exploitation.[71] Allegations have also been made that the Titanium Group properties have served as a haven for drug traffickers and other criminal elements. Titanium Group owner, Alejandro Iglesias Rebollo, became a fugitive from Mexican justice shortly after one of his nightclubs, the Lobohombo, burned down in October 2000, killing 22 people. Despite his status as a criminal fugitive, Iglesias continues to operate his criminal enterprise from an undisclosed location and was allowed to open a new nightclub in Mexico City in the summer of 2002.[72]

The Salman Saleh/Chen/Lin Organization

Between July 1999 and November 2001, this international alien smuggling and document forgery ring specialized in the smuggling of Chinese nationals into the United States through Ecuador and Mexico. The ring consisted of a network with nodes in Shoueng and Guang-Zou City, China; Mexico City; Houston; and Brooklyn, New York. Chinese nationals or their families had to pay a smuggling fee ranging from US$20,000 to US $30,000 before departing China. The ring also created and used counterfeit immigration documents (form I-551 – alien Registration Receipt Cards) for Chinese aliens. The documents were intended to legitimize the aliens' presence and facilitate their movement by airplane from Quito or Mexico into the United States. The leader of the ring in Mexico, Saleh Ahmad Salman, is currently serving a 20-year prison sentence for human smuggling.[73]

The Heredia Organization "Airport Cartel"

This organization, which derives its name from its operations at Tijuana's international airport, is considered to be one of the Mexico's largest and most sophisticated alien smuggling rings. Tijuana-based alien smuggler, Guillermo Isiordia Heredia and members of his extended family, head the ring. According to a January 2001 story in the Tijuana newspaper, *Frontera*, the Heredia organization escorts dozens of illegal migrants through the Tijuana airport on any given

---

[71] "Hungarian Ambassador Denounces Women Smuggling," *The News* [Mexico City], 26 November 2000.
[72] "Iglesias abre más centro nocturnes"[Iglesias Opens More Nightclubs], Especialistas en Medios, S.A. [Mexico City], 27 June 2002.
[73] U.S. Attorney's Office, Southern District of Texas, News Release, "Manager of International Alien Smuggling Ring Sentenced," 30 August 2002.

day.[74] The organization is known to smuggle illegal migrants from Central and South America, Europe, Asia and Africa into the United States, allegedly with the knowledge of corrupt Mexican officials. According to *Frontera*, the migrants are transported to a safe house in the neighborhood of Buena Vista, from where they are boarded onto commercial passenger buses belonging to the *Transportes Norte de Sonora* bus company en route to Nogales, Sonora. The migrants are subsequently crossed into the United States by means of a tunnel connecting Nogales, Mexico with Nogales, Arizona. A January 2003 story in the *Nogales International* indicates that alien smuggling activity was detected through the Nogales drainage tunnel system as recently as July 2002.[75] From Nogales, the migrants transported to Tucson and Los Angeles.

The "Manhattan Gang"

This Tijuana-based alien smuggling ring derives its name from the Hotel Manhattan in Tijuana, where many of the group's members are said to meet on a regular basis. According to local media accounts dating from early 2001, the gang, which is reportedly led by two brothers from the state of Jalisco, employs dozens of local smugglers and pickpockets who specialize in visa and passport theft. The group has a large cache of stolen passports and visa documents, which are matched to illegal migrants who resemble the original bearers.[76]

The "El Ramón" and "El Chiquito" Gang

Alien smugglers, Ramón Jiménez, alias El Ramón, and Luis Antonio Zúñiga, alias El Chiquito, lead this Tijuana-based alien smuggling ring. The group collaborates with local bus companies at Tijuana's central bus terminal to transport illegal migrants to the United States via bus. According to *Frontera*, their preferred route is the Mexicali-Calexico border crossing.[77]

---

[74] Jorge Morales, "Revelan operación y centros de tráfico de migrantes" [Migrant Trafficking Operations and Centers Revealed], *Frontera*, 3 January 2001.
<http://www.frontera.info/edicionimpresa/traernota.asp?NumNota=81885>
[75] "Border Drug Tunnel Was in Use From March Through July," *Nogales International*, 5 January 2003.
<http://www.nogalesinternational.com/>
[76] Morales.
[77] Morales.

The "El Libanés" Boughader Organization

The existence of this Tijuana-based alien smuggling ring, which specialized in the smuggling of Middle Eastern immigrants, was publicly revealed in January 2001.[78] The organization, which was led by Salim Boughader Mucharrafille, a Mexican of Lebanese decent, was disrupted in December 2002, when Boughader was taken into custody in San Diego on alien smuggling charges. According to a 16-count indictment, Boughader worked with two other Mexicans, Patricia Serrano Valdéz and José Guillermo Álvarez Dueñas, for at least a year to transport Middle Eastern immigrants across established smuggling routes through the San Ysidro Port of Entry and the mountains in East County.[79] According to *Frontera*, the ring charged migrants US$2,500 for the border crossing part of their journey. The Boughader organization is believed to have smuggled several dozen Iraqi Christians who were fleeing religious persecution in Iraq and intended to seek asylum in the United States. U.S. law enforcement agencies were concerned that potential terrorists could take advantage of the same routes.[80]

The "Smuggler M" Organization

This organization has smuggled large numbers of Egyptian and other Middle Eastern nationals into the United States via the U.S.-Mexico border. The smuggling ring flies undocumented Middle Eastern migrants to Brazil on tourist visas and subsequently takes them to Guatemala, from where they are clandestinely transported through Mexico and across the U.S. border. Many of those who have been smuggled by the group come from or have contacts with the Egyptian town of Bata, an impoverished community 20 miles north of Cairo. In May 2002, federal agents in New Jersey arrested two members of this smuggling ring, the brothers Adel R. Nasr and Gamal Abdalgalil Nasr, on immigration and alien smuggling charges. An unsealed indictment in the case stated that the two brothers worked with an unidentified Egyptian national based in Guatemala City identified only as "Smuggler M."[81]

---

[78] Morales.

[79] Marisa Taylor and Sandra Dibble, "Tijuana Man Charged with Heading up a Smuggle Ring," *San Diego Union-Tribune*, 14 December 2002.

[80] Joel Millman, "Promised Land: Why a Christian Iraqi Yearning for Detroit Landed in Mexican Jail," *Wall Street Journal*, 30 November 2001.

[81] Mitchel Maddux, "Two Accused of People Smuggling," *The Record* [Bergen County, New Jersey], 22 May 2002, A3.

FOREIGN TRANSNATIONAL CRIMINAL ORGANIZATIONS

Russian Organized Crime Groups

Interpol reports indicate that a variety of Russian criminal organizations, operating through dozens of small cells, are engaged in a wide range of illegal activities in Mexico.[82] Russian mafia groups such as the Poldolskaya, Mazukinskaya, Tambovskaya, and Izamailovskaya have been detected in Mexico.[83] The Moscow-based Solntsevskaya gang is also reported to be present in the country, as are other mafia gangs from Chechnya, Georgia, Armenia, Lithuania, Poland Croatia, Serbia, Hungary, Albania, and Rumania. Their major activities include drug and arms trafficking, money laundering, prostitution, trafficking in women from Eastern and Central Europe and Russia, alien smuggling, kidnapping, and credit card fraud.[84]

Russian criminal organizations have discovered that linkages with one or more of the seven principal Mexican criminal organizations allow them to obtain drugs at low prices and under relatively secure circumstances. In order to maintain a low profile, Russian mafia groups in Mexico often operate out of resorts, hotels, or houses protected and owned by their Mexican associates. Beginning in the late 1990s, the growing importance of the Pacific route as the most reliable maritime corridor for Colombian cocaine bound for Mexico created a demand for the types of open-sea transportation services that Russian mafia organizations were well positioned to provide.

During the summer of 1997, the Mexican media began to report widely on the ties between Russian Organized Crime (ROC) groups and Mexican polydrug trafficking organizations. According to these reports, Mexican drug traffickers established formal alliances with Russian organized crime groups as early as 1992.

In a July 1997 story, the Mexico City daily *Reforma* reported that narcotics kingpin Amado Carillo Fuentes had traveled to Moscow in February 1997 to explore the possibility of expanding his operations into Russia. The *Reforma* story also claimed that Russian and

---

[82] Gretchen Peters, "Drug Trafficking in the Pacific Has a Distinct Russian Flavor," *San Francisco Chronicle*, 30 May 2001.

[83] Bruce Michael Bagley, "Globalization and Transnational Organized Crime: The Russian Mafia in Latin America and the Caribbean," School of International Studies, University of Miami, 31 October 2001. <http://www.mamacoca.org/feb2002/art_bagley_globalization_organized_crime_en.html>

[84] Doris Gomora, "Las redes de la mafia globalizada en Mèxico" [The Networks of the Global Mafia in Mexico], *Reforma* [Mexico City], 16 May 2001, 9.

Armenian crime groups based in southern California had entered into distribution arrangements with Mexican drug traffickers in the mid-1990s.[85]

In December 1997, *Reforma* reported that U.S. intelligence agencies had detected a partnership between the Tijuana-based Arellano-Felix Organization (AFO) and Russian mafia groups based in southern California.[86] In a separate story, *Reforma* reported that members of the KGB-affiliated Kurganskaya group in San Diego had met with AFO operative Humberto Rodríguez Banuelos as early as January 1992.[87]

In February 1998, *Reforma* reported that the Russian mafia was supplying Mexican drug traffickers with radars, automatic weapons, grenade launchers, and small submersibles in exchange for cocaine, amphetamines, and heroin. It cited a 1996 sting operation in which undercover DEA agents posing as Russian mafia members sold Carillo Fuentes operatives 300 AK-47s and ammunition in Costa Rica.[88]

In July 1997, ten Russians, including four known members of the Russian mafia, were arrested at Mexico City's international airport when they arrived on a KLM flight from Amsterdam. The mafia members included Aleksandr Zakharov, one of the leaders of the Moscow mafia and founder of the Uralinvest, known to have a principal role in organized crime in Russia. Another detainee was Nicolay Novikov, a Uralinvest director who had been imprisoned on three previous occasions for arms trafficking. A third was Yevgeniy Sazhayev, who had been arrested on two previous occasions for drug trafficking. The fourth was Vladimir Titov, wanted for various assassinations and who had escaped from several Russian prisons with the help of the mafia. The four men, who were traveling with six women, were apparently en route to Acapulco and Cancún. The group was reportedly deported. The Interpol head in Mexico, Juan Manuel Ponce, corroborated accounts that the group had been carrying arms and a substantial amount of cash.

According to Mexican analyst Jorge Fernández Méndez, the Russian mafia bosses had come to Mexico in order to mediate in the gang war being fought between the CFO and various other groups for control of drug trafficking routes through Mexico in the wake of the death of

---

[85] Alejandro Paez, "Buscaba Amado nexos con rusos" [Amado Sought Links to Russians], *Reforma* [Mexico City], 28 July 1997, 1.

[86] "Versión confirmada" [Report Confirmed], *Reforma* [Mexico City], 7 December 1997, 1.

[87] Inder M. Bugarin, "De Moscú a Tijuana" [From Moscow to Tijuana], *Reforma* [Mexico City], 7 December 1997, 26.

[88] Inder M. Bugarin. "Arma la mafia rusa a narcos mexicanos [The Russian Mafia Arms Mexican Drug Traffickers], *Reforma* [Mexico City], 3 February 1998, 1.

Amado Carillo Fuentes.[89] Fernández Méndez claims that the Russians were invited to Mexico by Enrique González Quirarte, a lieutenant of Carillo Fuentes who had been put in charge of negotiations with the Russian mafia.

During the spring of 2001, the seizure of approximately 19 tons of cocaine from two fishing boats manned by Russian and Ukrainian crewmen further raised concerns that Mexican drug smugglers are doing business with the Russian mafia. In March 2001, U.S. authorities seized between seven and eight tons of cocaine hidden on the ship *Forever My Friend*, manned by a crew of eight Russians and Ukrainians. In May 2001, the 152-foot Belize-flagged ship *Zvezda Maru*, carrying about 12 tons of cocaine, was towed to San Diego after it was intercepted by the Coast Guard on the high seas in the country's largest-ever maritime drug seizure. The *Zvezda Maru* and its crew of 12 Russians and Ukrainians were taken into custody after U.S. Coast Guard officials discovered cocaine in a secret compartment beneath the ship's holds. At the time of the *Zvezda Maru* bust, the DEA's San Diego chief, Errol Chávez, stated that the nationalities of the crew were an "indication that there is direct involvement or some kind of association between Russian organized crime and members of the Arellano-Felix organization."[90]

Ukrainian Criminal Organizations

Ukrainian criminal organizations have used Mexico as staging area for human smuggling activities directed at the United States. One such smuggling ring, which was broken up in May 2001, lured hundreds of Ukrainians—including women forced into prostitution—to Los Angeles and several other U.S. cities.[91] The ring, which charged up to US$7,500 per person, generated hundreds of thousands of dollars in illegal profits for its organizers.[92] The Ukrainian smugglers allegedly gave instructions to the illegal immigrants on what to tell U.S. Border Patrol agents if they got caught and how to walk across the U.S.-Mexican border. Tetyana Komisaruk, the alleged ringleader, was in charge of the inflow of trafficked Ukrainians and collecting payment from them. Her husband, Valery Komisaruk, "helped operate staging points in Mexico" that

---

[89] Jorge Fernández Méndez, *Narcotráfico y poder* (Mexico City: Rayuela Editores S.A. de C.V., 1999), 78.
[90] Peters. <http://sfgate.com/cgi-bin/article.cgi?file=/chronicle/archive/2001/05/30/MN165135.DTL>
[91] Josh Meyer, "11 Held in Immigrant Smuggling Operation," *Los Angeles Times*, 4 May 2001, B1.
[92] Federal Bureau of Investigation, Los Angeles Field Office, Press Release, "19 Linked to Eurasian Crime Ring Named in Federal Complaint for Alien Smuggling," 3 May 2001.
<http://www.losangeles.fbi.gov/2001/050301aliensmug.htm>

included a villa near the California border where the trafficked Ukrainians were housed until they arrived in the United States. The third key player was Serhiy Mezherytsky, a Ukrainian immigrant who once ran unsuccessfully for a seat on the city council in West Hollywood. He provided boats and cars for smuggling illegal immigrants and allegedly cooperated with Mexican guides to traffic smuggled immigrants into the United States.

Asian Organized Crime Groups

Asian criminal organizations are known to be active in Mexico as partners with domestic alien smuggling and human trafficking rings, as suppliers of primary materials for narcotics to Mexican drug traffickers, and as wholesalers and retailers of counterfeit merchandise and pirated intellectual property. Chinese and Japanese criminal networks have been frequently linked to Mexican alien smuggling rings operating in the northern states of Baja California Norte and Sonora. Asian criminal groups have also partnered with Mexican drug traffickers as suppliers of the precursor materials for synthetic drugs such as such as ephedrine.

Japanese Yazuka Gangs

In the spring of 1996, Mexican police broke up an organized crime ring that worked with Japanese Yazuka gangs to lure 1,200 young Mexican women to Japan over a 14-month period.[93] The women were told that they would be singers or actresses in Japan, but were forced into prostitution upon their arrival by Yazuka crime syndicates. Tijuana-based criminal organizations were believed to be operating with Japanese Yazuka gangs during this operation.

Chinese "Snakeheads"

Chinese alien smuggling organizations based in Fujian province work closely with Mexican alien smugglers to transport illegal Chinese migrants into the United States through Mexico. Fukinese "snakeheads" smuggle Chinese aliens through Mexico by several means. In some cases, cargo ships carrying hundreds of migrants have been offloaded near the Baja peninsula town of Ensenada. The migrants are handed off to Mexican border smuggling gangs who transport their human contraband by land in small groups to the Baja capital of Mexicali.

---

[93] Gregory Gross, "Mexican Women Forced to Be Sex Slaves: Taken to Japan, They Were Victimized by Organized Crime," *San Diego Union-Tribune*, 3 May 1996, A-1.

The Chinese migrants are able to blend in temporarily among Mexicali's large Mexican-Chinese population as they await opportunities to cross the U.S. border. The use of this route appears to have declined since the latter half of 1999, when Mexican authorities intercepted nearly 400 Chinese migrants who had been offloaded in the Ensenada area.[94] According to some U.S. observers, alien smugglers have paid tolls to the Arellano Felix drug trafficking organization, which controls much of the criminal activity on the Baja peninsula.[95] The Peralta-Rodríguez alien smuggling organization is also believed to be active in the Chinese human smuggling trade.

Another Chinese smuggling route, documented by the Mexico City daily *La Jornada*, involves landings in Mazatlán, in the western state of Sinaloa. From Sinaloa the migrants are taken to Hermosillo in the state of Sonora, where they are transferred to Sonora-based smuggling gangs. The migrants are eventually taken to the smuggling center of Agua Prieta, across from Douglas, Arizona. Once over the U.S. border, *La Jornada* reports that Chinese migrants are transported to California, Illinois, New York, and Washington state.[96]

A third Mexican route for Chinese migrant smugglers was documented in the May 2000 issue of *Time Asia*.[97] This route involves the offloading of Chinese migrants on sandbars off the Pacific coast of Guatemala. The migrants are then picked up in small boats by Taiwanese gangsters and taken to Guatemala City. In Guatemala City, a witness has described being taken to the property of a wealthy Taiwanese man who is considered a "big boss." The migrants are then transported overland to the Mexican border and into the state of Chiapas, where they are handed off to armed Mexican *coyotes*. Once in Mexico, the migrants are put into tractor trailers and taken across Mexico on a 40-hour journey to a remote forest near the U.S. border to await crossing opportunities. According to a witness, the Chinese migrants were picked up on the U.S. side of the border by Chinese snakeheads. They were first taken to Houston and later to Los Angeles to arrange payment for their journey.

---

[94] Ken Ellingwood, "176 Chinese Held in Mexico With 6 Alleged Smugglers," *Los Angeles Times*, 29 June 1999, 3; and Ellingwood, "110 Chinese Immigrants Seized in Baja California, *Los Angeles Times*, 25 September 1999, 19.
[95] Jamie Dettmer, "Boatloads May Contain More than Immigrants," *Insight on the News* [Washington], 23 August 1999, 6.
[96] "Bandas internacionales de traficantes de indocumentados utilizan mar, cielo y tierra nacionales para internar chinos hacia territorio estadunidense" [International Human Trafficking Gangs Use Land, Air and the Mexican Territory to Smuggle Chinese Into the United States], *La Jornada* [Mexico City], 14 July 1996.
[97] Terry McCarthy, "Journey to the West," *Time Asia*, 8 May 2000.

The Korean Mafia

Recently, the "Korean mafia" has been identified in Mexico City as one of largest distributors of counterfeit products and pirated intellectual property illegally imported from Asia. In December 2002, Mexico's Federal Preventive Police launched a crackdown against Korean merchandise counterfeiters in Mexico City. The authorities raided 24 locations in the capital and confiscated 180 tons of counterfeit merchandise manufactured in China and Taiwan. During the operation, Mexican police arrested 43 Koreans, including alleged ringleaders Kookh Kim Sung Hol and Hyo Sun Park.[98]

DOMESTIC INSURGENT AND TERRORIST ORGANIZATIONS

Mexico's government officially recognizes the existence of just three insurgent groups, although the Secretariat of National Defense has identified as many as 16 guerrilla bands.[99] The best known is the Zapatista National Liberation Army (Ejército Zapatista de Liberación Nacional—EZLN), with which the government has had an uneasy truce since the insurgents staged a violent, short-lived 1994 revolt in the southern state of Chiapas. The other two are the People's Revolutionary Army (Ejército Popular Revolucionario--EPR), which operates mainly in Guerrero and Oaxaca states, and an EPR offshoot formed in 1998 called the Revolutionary Army of the Insurgent People (Ejército Revolucionario del Pueblo Insurgente—ERPI). Media reports indicate that as many as 25 insurgent groups may be active in the country. Except for the EZLN, most of the insurgent groups number no more than a few dozen to a few hundred militants. Several of the guerilla bands are recent offshoots of the Popular Revolutionary Army (EPR), a leftist insurgency based in the mountainous state of Guerrero.

Most of the guerrilla groups finance themselves by means of kidnapping rings that target prominent Mexicans for ransom. The EPR, for example, is believed to have netted US$30 million from a single kidnapping operation in 1994. It is not clear to what degree Mexico's insurgent groups may be active in drug trafficking, manufacture, or cultivation as a source of income. In an April 2000 report on the Mexican heroin trade, the DEA found no evidence to conclude that Mexico's two largest guerrilla groups, the Zapatista National Liberation Army

---

[98] Luis alegre, "Cae red de piratería; retienen a 43 coreanos" [Counterfeiting Network Dismantled; 43 Koreans Detained], *Reforma* [Mexico City], 6 December 2002, 22.
[99] Daniel Pensamiento "Alerta el Ejército contra la guerilla" [Army Issues Guerrilla Alert], *Reforma* [Mexico City] 29 November 1999, 1.

(EZLN) and Popular Revolutionary Army (EPR), were engaged in heroin trafficking.[100] However, in May 1999 army troops and state police in the Guerrero town of Ajuchitlán del Progreso captured two guerrillas who were guarding an opium poppy field. The captured guerrillas described themselves as members of an EPR breakaway faction, the Armed Ecologist Group (Grupo Ecologista Armado—GEA), and claimed they were growing poppies in order to fund arms purchases for the new organization. It is possible that the captured guerillas may have fabricated the organization name in order to deflect attention from EPR drug trafficking activity.[101]

The Zapatista National Liberation Army (EZLN)

The Zapatista National Liberation Army (Ejército Zapatista de Liberación Nacional—EZLN) is by far the largest and most sophisticated insurgent group in Mexico. This highly media-savvy organization is not a purely indigenous movement, but is instead an alliance of radicalized middle-class intellectuals and indigenous groups dating from the early 1980s. The EZLN began as an offshoot of the National Liberation Forces (Fuerzas de Liberación Nacional—FLN), a Maoist guerrilla group that had been largely dormant since the 1970s. At the start of the Zapatista rebellion, command of Zapatista forces was jointly held by FLN veterans from Mexico City and a "clandestine committee" of Chiapas Indians representing the various ethnic subgroups residing in the area. In early 1996, the Zapatistas declared their willingness in principle to lay down their arms and become a legal political party pending major reforms of the political system. By declaring an indefinite ceasefire and engaging in a prolonged process of negotiations with the government over indigenous rights laws, the organization shifted its focus from armed struggle to political mobilization of Mexico's largely indigenous underclass on behalf of land rights and against "globalization."

The EZLN's highly effective recruitment of an international support network of anti-globalization activists has earned it the title of world's first "post-communist" insurgency, while

---

[100] United States Drug Enforcement Administration, *The Mexican Heroin Trade*, April 2000 (DEA-20014). <http://www.usdoj.gov/dea/pubs/intel/20014/20014.html>
[101] Jesús Guerrero, "Confiesan campesinos ser del EPR" [Campesinos Admit EPR Membership], *El Norte* [Monterrey, Mexico], 10 May 1999, 2.

its strategy has been characterized as "social netwar."[102] Despite its preoccupation with projecting a nonviolent public image, the group remains armed and reserves the right of "self defense" if it believes that its existence or the livelihood of the indigenous groups it claims to represent are directly threatened.

Since the mid-1990s, armed EZLN militants have engaged in a continuous, low-intensity gang war with local paramilitary groups sponsored by ranchers and elements of the Institutional Revolutionary Party (Partido Revolucionario Institucioncal--PRI) in Chiapas. The violence, which has been largely confined to Chiapas, consists mainly of tit-for-tat shootings and acts of vandalism. Although the EZLN publicly eschews large-scale violence, there exists the possibility that dissatisfied urban cadres may at some point be drawn to more violent groups such as the EPR or ERPI. In the event that negotiations with the government were to stall or the physical or economic security of the Chiapas indigenous communities were to deteriorate significantly, it is conceivable that membership in the EZLN could become a gateway to future violent anti-system activity for thousands of EZLN supporters.

Popular Revolutionary Army (EPR)

The Popular Revolutionary Army (Ejército Popular Revolucionario–EPR) first emerged in Guerrero state in June 1996 as an alliance of 14 underground revolutionary groups. The guerilla alliance that gave birth to the EPR was a response to systematic police brutality against local villages in Guerrero, which culminated in the massacre of 18 peasants in the municipality of Coyuca de Benítez in June 1995. At the commemoration of the Coyuca de Benítez massacre in 1996, the EPR issued a "Manfesto of Aguas Blancas," which included a five-point statement of goals. The first objective was "overthrowing the antipopular, antidemocratic, demagogic and illegitimate government, which is at the service of national and foreign capital and the forces which sustain it, and for establishing a new government, essentially distinct from that which now holds power."[103] On August 7, 1996, at a clandestine news conference, EPR Comandante José Arturo called for a provisional revolutionary government that would reverse current free-market policies. It proposed overthrowing President Zedillo by force and reportedly distanced itself from

---

[102] David Rondfeldt and John Arquilla, "Emergence and Influence of the Zapatista Social Netwar," pages 171-199 in John Arquilla and David Rondfeldt, eds. *Networks and Netwars: The Future of Terror, Crime and Militancy* (Santa Monica: RAND, 2001). <http://www.rand.org/publications/MR/MR1382/>

[103] Mexican Labor News and Analysis, 2, no. 1, (7 January 1997). <http://www.ueinternational.org/vol2no1.html>

the Zapatistas' policies of negotiation and international pressure, employing a discourse "more reminiscent of the Marxism of 1970's guerrilla movements." José Arturo stated that the EPR had carried out bank robberies and kidnappings in order to finance itself, and that a new front had been forged in the Eastern Sierra.[104]

The EPR has been linked to the Clandestine Revolutionary Workers Party-Union of the People (PROCUP), a deep-underground remnant of the 1970s guerilla movement in Guerrero led by the radical schoolteacher, Lucio Cabas.[105] The PROCUP is suspected of having carried out the 1994 kidnapping of Mexican banking magnate Alfredo Harp Helu, who netted his captors a US$30 million ransom.[106] At the time of its emergence, many observers believed the EPR might become Mexico's version of Peru's Shining Path.

In August 1996, the group carried out a series of armed actions in six states killing more than a dozen police, soldiers, and others. According to a Department of Defense (DoD) report cited by the *Wall Street Journal*, by 1999 the EPR had clashed about 45 times with security forces in several Mexican states, causing about 100 casualties.[107]

The EPR is an intensely secretive organization, and charges of elitism and dogmatism against its leadership have led to several splinter factions in recent years, most notably the ERPI group [*see ERPI below*].[108] EPR cells have been identified in seven Mexican states and the Federal District (Mexico City). The areas of operation are believed to be México, Puebla, Morelos, Guerrero, Oaxaca, Veracruz, and Tabasco.[109] According to the 1999 DoD report, the EPR, which possesses AK-47 and AR-15 assault weapons, had about 500 combatants before the schism that gave birth to the ERPI.

In May 1999 army troops and state police in the Guerrero town of Ajuchitlán del Progreso captured two guerrillas who were guarding an opium poppy field. The captured guerrillas described themselves as members of a new EPR breakaway faction, the Armed

---

[104] "New Guerrilleros in Mexico: The EPR." < http://www.geocities.com/CapitolHill/3102/mb2_epr.html>

[105] Bill Weinberg, "Fire in the Sierra Madre, Mexico's Other Guerilla War." [undated]
<http://shadow.autono.net/sin001/mexico.htm>

[106] Misael Habana de los Santos, "El EPR, autor del secuestro de Alfredo Harp Helú en 1994" [The EPR Carried Out the Kidnapping of Alfredo Harp Helú in 1994], *Crónica* [Mexico City], 13 June 1998.

[107] José de Córdoba, "U.S. Sees Rebels as Posing a Threat to Mexican Vote," *Wall Street Journal*, 14 February 2000, A19.

[108] Bill Weinberg, "Drugs, Guerrillas, and Politicos in Mexico," *NACLA Report on the Americas*, 36, no. 2, (September/October 2002): 23.

[109] David Vicenteno and Jorge Arturo Hidalgo, "Preocupan guerrillas, pero no afectan al pais" [Guerrillas a Cause for Concern But Do Not Impact the Country], *Reforma* [Mexico City], 28 August 2001, 3.

Ecologist Group (Grupo Ecologista Armado—GEA), and claimed they were growing poppies in order to fund arms purchases for the new organization. It is possible that the captured guerillas may have fabricated the organization name in order to deflect attention from EPR drug trafficking activity.[110]

Revolutionary Army of the Insurgent People (ERPI)

The ERPI insurgent group is a offshoot of the EPR, which splintered off in January 1998. At the time of the schism, the breakaway faction accused the EPR leadership of being "dogmatic, anti-democratic, conservative and intolerant." At the time of its formation, the ERPI claimed to be building an "army of the people" that would be ready for a nation-wide insurrection in the year 2000.[111] This group operates mainly in the highlands of the Sierra Madre del Sur in Guerrero, state, but is also suspected of having cells in the states of Oaxaca, Puebla, and Morelos. Since 1998, the ERPI has engaged in at least four violent ambushes of military and police detachments in Guerrero. It may also have participated in the student takeover at the National Autonomous University of Mexico (UNAM) in Mexico City that took place from April 1999 to February 2000. According to the former director of Mexico's domestic intelligence agency, Jorge Tello Peón, ERPI is organized into six commands dispersed between Guerrero and Oaxaca.[112] The group finances itself mainly by kidnapping business executives and other prominent persons for ransom. The ERPI has actively sought to expand its ranks by recruiting radicalized student activists in Mexican universities, but it does not appear to be developing into a serious threat to security beyond the rural state of Guerrero.

Revolutionary Armed Forces of the People (FARP)

The Revolutionary Armed Forces of the People (Fuerzas Armadas Revolucionarias del Pueblo–FARP) is a splinter faction of the EPR, whose existence was first reported publicly in February 2000, when it detonated a pipe bomb outside a government building in Puebla. The FARP's pipe-bombing attacks, while so far causing no casualties and minimal damage, have

---

[110] Jesús Guerrero, "Confiesan campesinos ser del EPR" [Campesinos Admit EPR Membership] *El Norte* [Monterrey, Mexico], 10 May 1999, 2.
[111] Bill Weinberg, "Fire in the Sierra Madre, Mexico's Other Guerilla War."
[112] David Pavón, "Cronología del EPR y del ERPI (1998-1999)" *Revolución*, no. 25, (January 2000). <http://www.geocities.com/Pentagon/Bunker/5061/cron3.htm>

targeted U.S.-affiliated institutions, including a McDonalds restaurant and a General Motors automobile dealership near the Mexico City airport on September 1, 2001. In August 2001, the FARP bombed three branches of the Mexican bank, Banamex, in Mexco City, reportedly to protest its merger with Citigroup. That same month, the Mexican army announced it had dismantled a FARP cell in Mexico City and Mexico state consisting of five individuals, of whom three were students at the National Autonomous University of Mexico (UNAM).[113] The group funds itself by means of kidnapping and extorsion. According to media accounts citing a PGR intelligence estimate, FARP cells have been detected in the states of Guerrero and Morelos and in the Federal District (Mexico City).

Villista Revolutionary Army of the People (EVRP)

The Villista Revolutionary Army of the People (Ejército Villista Revolucionario del Pueblo–EVRP) is an EPR splinter faction that was established in December 1999 and is based in Guerrero. The group has claimed responsibility for a March 2000 attack against the headquarters of the Federal Preventive Police and the Santa Lucia air base in the state of México. It also claims to have participated in the September 1, 2001 attack against a General Motors dealership and a McDonalds restaurant near the Mexico City airport as part of the CGNJMMP umbrella organization.

Clandestine Revolutionary Committee of the Poor (CCRP-28J)

Little is known about the Clandestine Revolutionary Committee of the Poor (Comité Clandestino Revolucionario de los Pobres-Comando Justiciero 28 de Junio–CCRP-28J) an EPR splinter faction based in Guerrero. In March 2000, this group joined with the FARP and EVRP to form the José Maria Morelos y Pavón National Guerrilla Coordinating Group (Coordinadora Guerrillera Nacional José Maria Morelos y Pavón--CGNJMMP). It claims to have participated, along with the FARP and EVLN, in the September 1, 2001 pipe-bomb attacks against a McDonalds restaurant and a General Motors dealership near the Mexico City airport.[114]

---

[113] "Anuario 2001/Resurgen estallidos; eligen Banamex" [2001in Review: Bombings Return; Banamex Targeted], *Reforma* [Mexico City], 19 December 2001.
[114] "Contraataca guerrilla en el DF; declaran alerta en el aeropuerto," [Guerrillas Counterattack in the Federal District, Airport on State of Alert], *El Norte* [Monterrey, Mexico], 2 September 2001, 10.

The José Maria Morelos y Pavón National Guerrilla Council (CGNJMMP)

The José Maria Morelos y Pavón National Guerrilla Council (Coordinadora Guerrillera Nacional José Maria Morelos y Pavón –CGNJMMP) is an umbrella organization that groups together three small ERP breakaway groups: the FARP, EVRP, and the CCRP-28J. The CGNJMMP was announced in March 2001 and has claimed responsibility for the September 1, 2001 bombing attacks against a McDonalds restaurant and a General Motors dealership near the Mexico City airport.[115]

Popular Revolutionary Army-Democratic Revolutionary Tendency (EPR-TDR)

Little is known about the Popular Revolutionary Army-Democratic Revolutionary Tendency (Ejército Popular Revolucionario-Tendencia Democrática Revolucionaria—EPR-TDR) except that it is an EPR splinter faction based in the state of Guerrero.[116]

Popular Insurgent Revolutionary Army (ERIP)

The existence of the Popular Insurgent Revolutionary Army (Ejército Revolucionario Insurgente Popular–ERIP), which is not recognized by the Mexican government, has never been confirmed. A news release sent to Mexican media outlets in November 1996 declared the formation of an armed insurgency in northern Mexico. In a document titled "Declaration of the North," the authors claimed they were part of a popular army consisting of farmers, native Indians, city workers, professionals, poor retailers, and small nationalist businessmen who are exploited by "monopolistic groups serving transnational capital."[117] The press release, however, did not divulge a region from which the group supposedly operates nor any plans for military action. A February 1998 story in the Mexican daily *Reforma* speculated that Russian criminal organization cells based in San Diego may be providing weapons to the ERIP and another northern Mexican "insurgent" group.[118] However, the available open source literature contains no evidence to suggest that the ERIP is active anywhere in Mexico. Mexican observers have

---

[115] "Contraataca guerrilla en el DF; declaran alerta en el aeropuerto."

[116] Guadalupe Irizar, "Ubican siete grupos guerrilleros" [Seven Guerrilla Groups Identified], *El Norte* [Monterrey: Mexico], 22 July 2001, 7.

[117] "U.S. Government Says Mexico Failing in Drug Fight," *Dow Jones* [Mexico City], 21 November 1996.

[118] Inder M. Bugarin, "Mafia Rusia da Armas a Guerilla" [Russian Mafia Arms Guerillas], *Reforma* [Mexico City], 5 February 1998, 5.

suggested the ERIP may be a front for one or more criminal gangs operating in Mexico's "Golden Triangle," a narcotics cultivation zone in the states of Sinaloa, southern Sonora, Durango, and Nayarit.[119]

FOREIGN TERRORIST ORGANIZATIONS

Mexico's traditional foreign policy of "nonintervention" and its generous asylum practices toward refugees from Latin America's right-wing dictatorships historically made it a hospitable environment for radical organizations of the left. Since the 1970s, several Latin American guerilla and terrorist organizations have been allowed to maintain political delegations in Mexico City. In addition, hundreds of "demobilized" militants have been granted safe haven in the country under a general understanding that they are not to become involved with Mexico's domestic insurgencies or otherwise attempt to agitate among Mexico's large underclass. These radical political delegations have generally found Mexico City to be a convenient base for their fundraising activities and a safe haven from which to conduct propaganda and media events. Mexico has also served as host over the years to peace talks between various Latin American guerilla groups and their home governments.

In addition to this authorized presence, at least two terrorist groups have maintained a clandestine presence in Mexico. The Colombian FARC, for example, is believed to have established a covert drug trafficking relationship with the Arellano-Felix drug trafficking organization during the latter 1990s. Similarly, members of the Basque terrorist group Fatherland and Liberty (Euskadi Ta Askatasuna—ETA) have covertly taken up residence in Mexico in order to establish legitimate business enterprises used to fund their terrorist activities in Spain.

Revolutionary Armed Forces of Colombia (FARC)

Through its Mexico City office, the Revolutionary Armed Forces of Colombia (Fuerzas Armadas Revolucionarias de Colombia–FARC), Colombia's largest terrorist organization, maintained an overt, legally authorized presence in Mexico for more than a decade. The FARC's Mexico City office, staffed by Colombian militants Marco León Calarca and Olga Marín, was accepted by both the Mexican and Colombian governments as a useful point of contact for

---

[119] "Gobierno pone en duda existencia de tercer grupo armado" [Government Doubts Existence of Third Armed Group], *Inter Press Service* [Mexico City] 26 November 1996.

purposes of engaging in peace talks. It was also thought to be a potential source of intelligence about the FARC's international activities.[120] This legal presence of the FARC in Mexico came to an end in April 2002, when the Mexican government, at the request of Colombia, shut the office down and expelled Calarca and Marín from the country.

In addition to its official delegation in Mexico, it is now known that the FARC established a clandestine collaboration with the Tijuana-based Arellano Felix drug trafficking organization (AFO).[121] In August 2001, Mexican authorities arrested Colombian national Carlos Ariel Charry Guzmán in Mexico City on drug trafficking charges. In November, Charry Guzmán was charged with setting up a cocaine-for-arms deal with the AFO. Mariano Herran Salvatti, then Mexico's top drug prosecutor, said at the time that Charry Guzmán was working for senior FARC leader Briceno and was "the link, the coordinator of shipments of drugs and receiver of payments in money or arms" between the FARC and the AFO.[122] In March 2002, Mexican officials arrested Rigoberto Yannez, alias El Primo, allegedly a senior lieutenant in the Tijuana cartel who served as a go-between in the FARC deal.

Fatherland and Liberty (ETA)

The Basque terrorist organization Fatherland and Liberty (Euskadi Ta Askatasuna–ETA) has maintained a continuous presence in Mexico since 1963, when ETA co-founder José Manuel Aguirre took up residence in the country and established an official delegation.[123] The ETA presence in Mexico, which originally consisted of legal immigrants and asylum seekers, grew until the early 1990s, when an ETA plot to kidnap high ranking business executives from several countries, including Mexico, was uncovered. The Mexican government's tolerance of ETA was further eroded in 1994, when it was discovered that the Spanish terrorist group maintained close ties to the Zapatista (EZLN) rebel movement in Chiapas.

During 1996, ETA's leadership recommended that its cadres in Latin America voluntarily relocate to France. However, according to Mexican media, many of the ETA militants who left for France were replaced by new arrivals to Mexico. In July 1997, the Spanish and Mexican

---

[120] Daniel Millán, "Tuvieron las FARC oficina en Mexico" [The FARC Had an Office in Mexico], *Reforma* [Mexico City], 10 August 2002, 7.
[121] U.S. Department of State website, "Text: State Dept. on Colombian Rebel Connection to Mexican Drug Cartel," Washington, DC, 29 November 2000. <http://usinfo.state.gov/regional/ar/mexico/drug29.htm>
[122] T. Christian Miller, "Colombian Rebels Step Up Drug Trade Activity," *Houston Chronicle*," 17 June 2001, 29.
[123] Carlos Rubio, "Revela investigación la vida dentro de ETA," *Reforma* [Mexico City], 16 January 2002, 3.

media reported that at least 130 ETA members remained in Mexico. The Mexico City daily *Reforma* published the names and locations of 32 suspected ETA militants located in cities throughout the country. Since the mid-1990s, Mexico, at the request of the Spanish government, has deported scores of ETA militants to Spain. The largest concentrations of ETA members have been located in the northern city of Monterrey and in Mexico City. In May 2001, Mexican national security adviser Adolfo Aguilar Zinser confirmed that ETA continued to maintain a covert presence in the country and stated that more than 20 members of the group had been arrested in recent months. [124] ETA's activities in Mexico generally consist of establishing and managing legitimate business enterprises for purposes of fundraising and money laundering.

Islamic Terrorist Organizations

Statements made by high-ranking Mexican officials prior to and following the September 11, 2001 terrorist attacks indicate that one or more Islamic terrorist organizations has sought to establish a presence in Mexico. In May 2001, former Mexican national security adviser and current ambassador to the United Nations, Adolfo Aguilar Zinser, stated, that "Spanish and Islamic terrorist groups are using Mexico as a refuge… In light of this situation, there are continuing investigations aimed at dismantling these groups so that they may not cause problems in the country."[125] Asked by reporters for specific information, Zinser replied, "We have cases of many terrorist organizations that are seeking to set up refuges in Mexico. There are Islamic people. There are also people from ETA." [126] Aguilar noted that, despite the situation, "there are no indications that these terrorist groups may have established contact with Mexican organizations." He also mentioned that the terrorist groups in question had been located in the northern part of the country and were shifting operations toward the south but did not elaborate. Prior to September 11, Zinser's remarks about "Islamic people" in Mexico sparked speculation among observers that the Lebanese Shi'ite terrorist organization Hizbollah may have established cells in Mexico.[127] A Hizbollah presence in northern Mexico was considered a possibility by

---

[124] "Mexican Official Says Spanish, Islamic "Terrorist Groups" Use Mexico as Refuge," *BBC Monitoring /Notimex*, 30 May 2001.
[125] "Mexican official says Spanish, Islamic "Terrorist Groups" Use Mexico as Refuge," *BBC Monitoring /Notimex*, 30 May 2001.
[126] "Mexican Official Says Spanish, Islamic "Terrorist Groups" Use Mexico as Refuge."
[127] "Mexico Arrests Members of Terrorist Groups," *Special Warfare*, 14, no. 2 (Spring 2001). <http://www.call.army.mil/fmso/sof/issues/spring01.htm>

observers because of the sizable ethnic Lebanese and Palestinian communities in the northern Mexican city of Monterrey.[128]

Following the September 11 attacks, the focus of speculation shifted toward a possible al Qaeda presence in Mexico.[129] Remarks made by Mexican public officials in the aftermath of the attacks addressed the possibility that al Qaeda cells could be present in Mexico and could potentially attempt to cross the U.S. southwest border to conduct additional attacks.

In October 2001, during a UN conference, the director of Mexico's Center for Intelligence and National Security (Centro de Inteligencia y Seguridad Nacional—Cisen), Eduardo Medina Mora, remarked that the possibility of an al Qaeda attack against the United States launched from Mexico "could not be ruled out."[130] However, Medina Mora stated that Cisen had no reason to believe that there was an al Qaeda presence in Mexico.

In January 2002, National Migration Institute (Instituto Nacional de Migracion—INM) official Felipe Urbiola Ledezma made more alarming were statements. During remarks to the press, Urbiola said, "We have in Mexico people linked to terrorism and we are constantly observing unusual immigration flows…[people connected to] ETA, Hizbollah and even some with links to Usama Bin Laden." [131] He added that "there are six or seven organizations, but these are people who have links to them [terrorist groups] and are not themselves engaging in terrorist activities"[132] Urbiola's remarks were immediately disavowed by the INM, which issued a press release stating that "The National Migration Institute categorically denies statements made by officials of this organization in which it is alleged that foreign terrorist organizations or activities are being carried out in the national territory." [133]

---

[128] According to the Monterrey based daily, *El Norte*, there are about 400,000 Arabic speakers in Mexico; "Jessica Castañeda, "Habla usted…arabe?" [Do You Speak Arabic?], *El Norte* [Monterrey, Mexico], 6 September 2002, 1.
[129] Graham H. Turbiville, "Potential Terrorist Entry to U.S. Along SW Border," *Special Warfare*, 15, no. 1 (Winter 2002): 45.
[130] Daniel Millán Valencia and Ernesto Nuñez, "Alerta Cisen de ataques por frontera con Mexico" [Cisen Raises Alert Over Attacks Through Mexican Border], *El Norte* [Monterrery, Mexico], 25 October 2001, 4.
[131] Fernando Paniagua, "Encuentran en Mexico vínculos con al-Qaeda" [Mexican Links to Al-Qaeda Discovered], *El Norte* [Monterrey, Mexico], 18 January 2002, 1.
[132] Paniagua.
[133] Paniagua.

APPENDIX

Map 1. Mexican Drug Trafficking Organizations: Areas of Influence

Map 1. Mexican Drug Trafficking Organizations: Areas of Influence

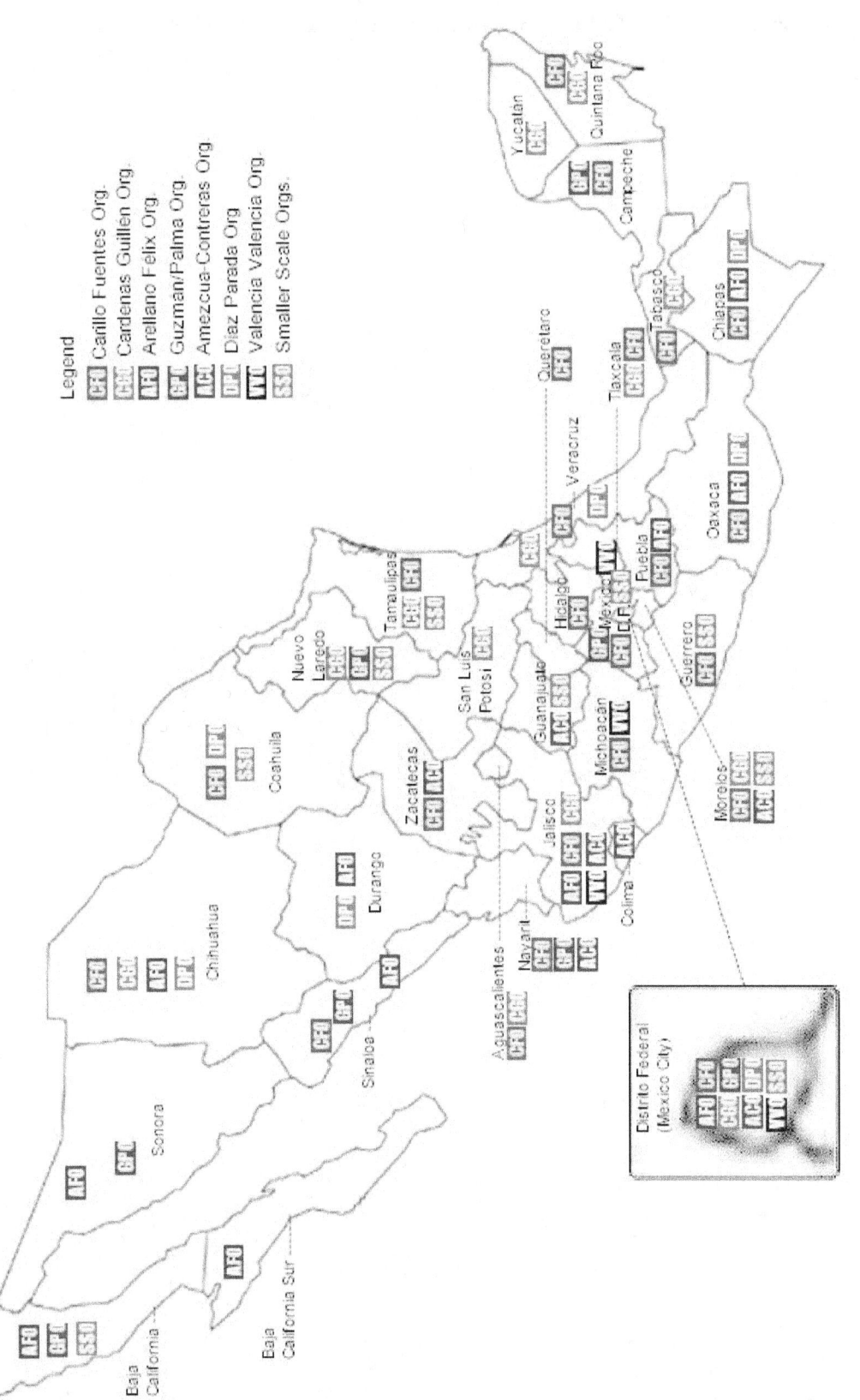

46

BIBLIOGRAPHY

Andreas, Peter. "The Political Economy of Narco-Corruption in Mexico," *Current History*, 97, No. 618, (April 1998), 160-65.

Andreas, Peter. "The Transformation of Migrant Smuggling Across the U.S.-Mexican Border." Pages 107-25 in David Kyle and Rey Koslowski, eds., *Global Human Smuggling: Comparative Perspectives*. Baltimore: Johns Hopkins University Press, 2001.

Bagley, Bruce Michael. "Globalization and Transnational Organized Crime: The Russian Mafia in Latin America and the Caribbean." Miami: University of Miami, School of International Studies, 31 October 2001.
<http://www.mamacoca.org/feb2002/art_bagley_globalization_organized_crime_en.html

Bailey, John, and Jorge Chabat, eds. *Transnational Crime and Public Security: Challenges to Mexico and the United States*. San Diego: Center for U.S.-Mexican Studies, University of California, 2002.

Bailey, John, and Roy Godson, eds. *Organized Crime and Democratic Governability: Mexico and the U.S.-Mexico Borderlands*. Pittsburgh: University of Pittsburgh Press, 2000.

Berry, Laverle, Glenn E. Curtis, Rex A. Hudson, and Nina A. Kollars. *A Global Overview of Narcotics-Funded Terorist and Other Extremist Groups*. Washington: Library of Congress, Federal Research Division, May 2002.

Carvajal Dávila, ed. *Todo lo que Debería Saber Sobre el Crimen Organizado en México*. Mexico City: Editorial Oceano, 1998.

Ciluffo, Frank J. "The Threat Posed from the Convergence of Organized Crime, Drug Trafficking, and Terrorism," Statement to the Subcommittee on Crime, U.S. House of Representatives, December 13, 2000.

Garrastazu, Antonio, and Jerry Haar. "International Terrorism: The Western Hemisphere Connection." Miami: University of Miami, North-South Center, 10 October 2001.
<http://www.miami.edu/nsc/pages/newsupdates/Update48.html>

Gobierno de Mexico, Procuradoría General de la República. *Programa Nacional para el Control de Drogas 2001-2006*. Mexico City: 2002. <http://www.pgr.gob.mx>

Graver, David. "Drug Money Laundering in Mexico." Pages 39-81 in William Cartwright, ed., *Mexico: Facing the Challenges of Human Rights and Crime*. Ardsley, New York: Transaction, 2000.

Holden-Rhodes, J.F. *Sharing the Secrets: Open Source Intelligence and the War on Drugs*. Westport, Connecticut: Praeger, 1997.

Hudson, Rex A. *An Overview of the Nexus Among the Russian Mafia and the Colombian Drug Cartels and Guerrilla Groups*. Washington: Library of Congress, Federal Research Division, January 2002.

Kaihla, Paul. "The Technology Secrets of Cocaine Inc.," *Business 2.0*, July 2002. <http://www.business2.com/articles/mag/0,1640,41206,00.html>

Kenney, Michael. "The Challenge of Eradicating Transnational Criminal Networks: Lessons from the War on Drugs." Paper delivered at the 2002 Annual Meeting of the American Political Science Association, Boston, 29 August – 1 September 2002.

Kenney, Michael. *Outsmarting the State: A Comparative Case Study of the Learning Capacity of Colombian Drug Trafficking Organizations and Government Counter-Narcotics Agencies*. Unpublished PhD. dissertation. Gainesville: University of Florida, 2002.

Klerks, Peter. "The Network Paradigm Applied to Criminal Organisations: Theoretical Nitpicking or a Relevant Doctrine for Investigators?" *Connections*, 24, no.3 (winter 2001): 53-65. <http://www.sfu.ca/~insna/Connections-Web/Volume24-3/klerks.pdf>

Leiken, Robert S. "War on Terror: Mexico More Critical Than Ever for U.S," *Sacramento Bee*, 24 March 2002.

Milward, H. Brinton. "Dark Networks: The Structure, Operation, and Performance of International Drug, Terror, and Arms Trafficking Networks." Paper presented at the International Conference on the Empirical Study of Governance, Management, and Performance, Barcelona, Spain, 4-5 October 2002. <http://www.iigov.org/workshop/pdf/Milward_and_Raab.pdf>

Poppa, Terrence. *Drug Lord: The Life and Death of a Mexican Kingpin*. Seattle: Demand Publications, 1998.

Rondfeldt, David, and John Arquilla. "Emergence and Influence of the Zapatista Social Netwar." Pages 171-99 in John Arquilla and David Rondfeldt, eds., *Networks and Netwars: The Future of Terror, Crime and Militancy*. Santa Monica, CA: RAND, 2001. <http://www.rand.org/publications/MR/MR1382/>

Rondfeldt, David, and John Arquilla. *The Zapatista "Social Netwar" in Mexico*. Santa Monica: RAND, 1998.

Smith, Paul J. "Transnational Terrorism and the al Qaeda Model: Confronting New Realities," *Parameters*, Summer 2002, 33-46.

Spener, David. "Smuggling Migrants Through South Texas: Challenges Posed by Operation Rio Grande." Pages 129-65 in David Kyle and Rey Koslowski, eds., *Global Human Smuggling: Comparative Perspectives*. Baltimore: Johns Hopkins University Press, 2001.

United States Congress.107th, 1st Session. House of Representatives. Committee on the Judiciary. *Drug Trafficking on the Southwest Border.* Washington: GPO, 29 March 2001. <http://www.house.gov/judiciary>

United States. Department of Justice. Drug Enforcement Administration. *Drug Intelligence Brief: Mexico Country Brief*, July 2002.

United States. Department of Justice. Drug Enforcement Administration. *Extraditable Mexican Traffickers* (DEA-99011), September 1999.

United States. Department of Justice. Drug Enforcement Administration. *The Mexican Heroin Trade* (DEA-20014), April 2000.

United States. Department of State. *International Narcotics Control Strategy Report: 2001.* Washington: GPO, March 2002.

Weinberg, Bill. "Drugs, Guerrillas and Politicos in Mexico," *NACLA Report on the Americas,* 36, no. 2 (September/October 2002): 18-26.

Williams, Phil. "The Nature of Drug Trafficking Networks," *Current History,* 97, no. 618 (April 1998): 154-59.

Williams, Phil. "Transnational Criminal Networks." Pages 61-97 in John Arquilla and David Rondfeldt, eds., *Networks and Netwars: The Future of Terror, Crime and Militancy.* Santa Monica, CA: RAND, 2001.

(Various issues of the following publications and several websites were also used in the preparation of this report: *Arizona Republic* [Phoenix, AZ]; *Chicago Tribune*; *Crónica* [Mexico City]; *El Norte* [Monterrey, Mexico]; *El Universal* [Mexico City]; *Frontera* [Tijuana]; *Houston Chronicle*; *Los Angeles Times*; *Milenio* [Mexico City]; *The News* [Mexico City]; *Nogales International* [Nogales, AZ]; *Reforma* [Mexico City]; Government of Mexico, Office of the Attorney General of the Republic [www.pgr.gob.mx]; and *San Diego Union-Tribune*).